WRESTLING
FUNDAMENTALS & TECHNIQUES
THE IOWA HAWKEYES' WAY

● **Foreword by Dan Gable**

by
Mark Mysnyk
University of Iowa

LEISURE PRESS
CHAMPAIGN, ILLINOIS

Published by Leisure Press
A Division of Human Kinetics Publishers, Inc.
Box 5076, Champaign, IL 61825-5076
1-800-747-4457
UK Office:
Human Kinetics Publishers (UK) Ltd.
P.O. Box 18
Rawdon, Leeds LS19 6TG
England
(0532) 504211
Copyright © 1982 by Mark Mysnyk
All rights reserved. Printed in the U.S.A.

ISBN 0-918438-98-5
Library of Congress Number: 81-83015
Text photos by Don Roberts
Cover photo by John McIvor, courtesy of the
Cedar Rapids Gazette
Many of the action photos are courtesy
of Chuck and Diane Yesalis

CONTENTS

ACKNOWLEDGEMENTS

The moves described in this book were originally collected as a notebook for the Iowa Intensive Wrestling Camp. Several Iowa wrestlers and coaches have contributed to them, but J. Robinson's coaching is reflected more than anyone else's in these moves. I would like to thank all of these wrestlers, and especially the individuals pictured below and on page 5, who gave their time and effort to complete the photographs included in this book. I would also like to thank Dan Gable, both for his coaching and his guidance.

Mark Mysnyk

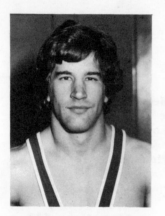

Tim Cysewski

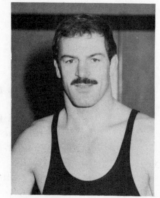

Lanny Davidson

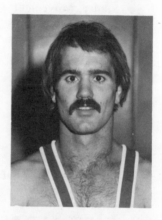

Garret Headley

Steve Kilwein

Randy Lewis

Keith Mourlam

Dan Gable

J. Robinson

Mark Mysnyk

THE AUTHOR

- Wrestled on four of the University of Iowa's NCAA championship teams.
- Alternate on the 1976 U.S. Olympic wrestling team.
- Member of the 1977 World University team.

FOREWORD

If anyone can capture the essence of championship wrestling, Mark Mysnyk is the one who will do it. Of the young wrestlers with whom I've been associated, this man has a knack for knowing what is important, when and where. The material contained in this book has been proven to work under tough conditions; mastering it is essential in competitive wrestling. The goal of every coach should be to teach the proper execution of skills to his athletes. There are few wrestling books that stress the best technique available in terms of best position. Because of Mark's closeness to our program at the University of Iowa, he has emphasized the positioning that will make each of the techniques described in this book work efficiently and effectively. This is a necessity in top-flight competition. Mark has outlined several alternatives to situations regarding accepted techniques—a bench-mark of real knowledge and the basis of **winning wrestling.** This book will be of great benefit to the dedicated wrestler.

Dan Gable

USING THIS BOOK

This book has been written as if it is directly coaching the wrestler reading it. In each of the photographs, the wrestler in the darker, Iowa uniform is the wrestler doing the move. As you study each move, you should not concentrate on that move alone, but also on what situations and other moves will set up that move. The names of the moves used in this book also need clarification. In different parts of the country (and even in the same area), some moves have several different names. No attempt has been made to include all of these names, and frequently a move is not named at all. Therefore when reading this book, the reader should realize that the name of a move is not that important, that it has nothing to do with whether the move works or not, and that some of the names in this book are inevitably different from what the reader thinks they should be.

INTRODUCTION

The University of Iowa's wrestling "style" could never be totally captured on paper. In the first place, there is not one style that explains Iowa wrestling. Each of the ten wrestlers who went to the NCAA's, each of the other thirty wrestlers in the practice room, and each of the coaches has his own style. In the second place, any book attempting to contain all the moves thrown by Iowa wrestlers would have to put out daily supplements, since new moves are learned daily. Whether it comes from Dan Gable, J. Robinson, or Chuck Yagla—certainly one of the finest coaching staffs in the country—or whether it comes from any of the wrestlers as they are working out, new set-ups, finishes, and even new moves surface constantly.

But while it's not possible to define Iowa's wrestling style, it is possible to explain its philosophy. Iowa wrestlers are coached to attack their opponents for the entire match—not with reckless abandon, but with a **series** of moves that have been set up. If one move doesn't work, a wrestler should change to a second move that the opponent opened up for in the process of countering the first move. If he counters the second move, a third move should be tried, and so on. This is chain wrestling, and it doesn't just apply to takedowns, but to every phase of wrestling.

The goal of this book is to make the reader aware of many different ways to chain moves together. Depending on how an opponent reacts, certain set-ups, moves, and finishes won't work, but there are others that will. This book approaches moves that way—several different set-ups, several finishes, and several different ways a move can fit into a chain of moves will be described for each move. Not only are the key points in each move emphasized, but so too are the most common mistakes that should be avoided. The counters to several moves are covered in similar detail.

No wrestler is expected to be able to do all of the moves in this book well enough to use them in a match. As explained above, this book represents numerous different styles. Each of the moves, though, is a proven move that has proven successful for at least one Iowa wrestler. The reader should experiment with each of these moves in the practice room and find out for himself which ones will best fit into his style. Whatever move is attempted, though, the wrestler should always be aware of the different ways of setting up and finishing that move, plus what options he has, depending on how the opponent reacts. Once the wrestler has devoted enough time and effort to his practice, the new moves will become instinctive.

1
THE BASIC COMPONENTS OF WRESTLING

Wrestling has four basic components: psychological, conditioning, strength, and technique. It is very difficult to rank these in order of importance, since being strong in any one or two of these aspects can compensate for weaknesses in the other areas, and exceptional strength in any one of these can produce a champion. This book concentrates on technique, but the other three aspects will be examined briefly here along with technique.

The first of these to be discussed—the psychological aspect—is probably the least understood and hardest to explain. This does not mean, however, that it is not important, for experts in all sports are recognizing the major role of the mind. It would take an entire book to explain completely what an optimal frame of mind is and how it is attained. This description will only attempt to introduce the topic and make the reader aware of it.

The first psychological component is confidence. This is *essential* for all athletes. A successful wrestler doesn't have to be continually bragging to others about how good he is, but inside himself he should be one hundred per cent convinced that he is the better wrestler each time he competes and that there is no way he can lose. It's important to be aware of an opponent's best moves, but you should never let his strengths dominate the match. Make him adjust to *your* style, not the other way around.

A second mental component can vaguely be described as "rising to the occasion." It is typified by the wrestler who in the last thirty seconds of a tough match always seems to wrestle better and score the necessary points. It is also what allows a wrestler to keep calm when things go wrong or he suddenly finds himself behind. A lot of this depends on confidence, knowing that one way or another you *are* going to win; but a major part is intangible and can only be developed by experience. A third aspect, here called "mental toughness" for lack of a better term, involves reaching "inside" and finding that extra strength when your mind is telling your body it's too tired to go on. This is discussed further in the conclusion.

The psychological component cannot be isolated from the other three aspects of wrestling and can significantly improve each of them. Performing a move with confidence is often more effective than doing the same move with better techniques but without confidence. Similarly, being able to ignore the fatigue and weakness that invariably come near the end of the match and "suck up" that extra effort can greatly increase the conditioning and strength **potential** of a wrestler without his running a single step or lifting a single weight.

The second component to be discussed—conditioning—is one over which that the wrestler has *total* control. There is no excuse for losing a match because of fatigue. The last paragraph described how mental toughness can increase a wrestler's conditioning potential, but this alone is not enough. The key to improving conditioning is simply hard work.

Hard wrestling is probably the best way of developing the conditioning needed for wrestling. You should wrestle as long as you can, take a short break, then wrestle again. As the season progresses, you should increase the time of each wrestling period, increase the total workout time, and decrease the rest time between periods. A second workout each day, including running, calisthenics, or weight lifting, should also be used to improve your conditioning. It's important to use your imagination and vary your workouts so they don't get boring. It's also important to stress the quality and not the quantity of the workout. Thirty minutes of intense work is far better than an hour of simply going through the motions and never getting tired.

Conditioning also improves the other three aspects of wrestling. As you feel your opponent tire, your confidence grows and his often disappears. Without conditioning, strength quickly diminishes, meaning that a conditioned but weak wrestler will become effectively stronger than his out-of-shape opponent as the match progresses. Similarly, if your opponent is considerably more tired than you are, all of your moves will be more effective than they were when your opponent was fresh.

Unlike the case with conditioning, a wrestler does not have total control over his strength. Every wrestler has a different natural body build, and while some can increase their strength faster than others, no one can improve his strength as fast as conditioning can be improved. This is not to say that strength is not important, since it is a major part of wrestling and every wrestler should work to increase it.

There are many different philosophies about how to lift weights, and while some methods are certainly better than others, any program worked at hard and regularly will do the job. You should lift hardest during the off-season, at least three times a week. During the season

Conditioning is the one component of wrestling over which the wrestler has total control.

Hard wrestling is probably the best way to develop the conditioning needed for wrestling.

Every wrestler must learn what moves work best for him, develop his own style, then continually add to it in order to make his wrestling more and more effective.

lifting is still important, but the workouts should be a little lighter and only two to three times a week with two to three days rest before meets.

As with the conditioning and psychological aspects of wrestling, strength can also add to all the other components. Knowing you can physically control your opponent should add to your confidence and take away from his. An intense weight lifting workout is a conditioner in itself, and increased strength can improve the technique you already have, make new moves possible, and limit the moves your opponent can do.

The final component, technique, is what this book concentrates on. There is a natural component to technique that involves both balance and agility. The major part, however, is directly under the control of the wrestler and simply involves a lot of time and work. Drilling is an essential part of every wrestler's workouts. Your drilling should be slow when you are first learning a move. Once you've learned it, though, you should drill hard, hitting each move just as you would in a match, including set-ups and finishes. Besides drilling, it is also important to get into specific situations and wrestle hard from there. Experience is important—you learn a specific position by wrestling from there over and over again. When wrestling hard in practice you shouldn't be afraid to try new moves. Although you should never get into the habit of giving away points, it doesn't mean a thing to get taken down in practice. Similarly if while practicing you find yourself in a situation where you're in trouble, don't try to get off the mat or give him the take down rather than fighting it. If it's a position with which you're having trouble, you need to learn that position better. Eliminate your mistakes in the practice room so that when you get into the same position in a match and can't get off the mat, you will know what to do.

The specific technique a wrestler uses is an individual decision. There are many different styles for the feet and on the mat, and all can be effective. Each wrestler must learn what moves work best for him, develop his own style, then continually add to it in order to make his wrestling more and more effective. If a move isn't working, analyze why it isn't. You could be doing the move wrong or else need to use a different set-up or finish. And as we stressed in the introduction, learning to chain moves together is very important. Even if the first move doesn't work it will usually set the opponent up for a second move, and it keeps him on the defensive.

As your technique improves, you will need less energy and strength to do each move, therefore conserving your conditioning and strength. Also, each time you score on an opponent it adds to your confidence and subtracts from his.

Clearly, then, the psychological, conditioning, strength, and technique components of wrestling are all interrelated. As mentioned earlier, it is hard to say which of these four is most important. Yet even if they could be ranked, that wouldn't change the fact that they are all important and that every wrestler should work to improve each of them.

2
BASIC SKILLS

Each of the basic skills is a key part of several other moves. Before these other moves are learned, every wrestler should master the following skills.

Stance, Movement

Whether you use a staggered or a square stance, there are certain key points that apply to both: you should be on the balls of your feet, *not* on your heels. **(2-1)** Before you move forward or shoot, and before you back up or sprawl, you must shift your weight to the balls of your feet. This takes extra time, and although it's only a short time, it may be the difference between success and failure. When you move, you should take *short* steps, stay on the balls of your feet, and never cross your legs. Your knees should be slightly bent, and your back should be straight, *not* bent over. If you're leaning forward it's easy for the man to snap you down. Your elbows should be in close to your side; otherwise you're open for fireman's carries, duck under, etc. Lastly, your hands should be in front on you so you can stop your opponent if he shoots in.

Figure 2-1

Penetration Step

This step, with slight variations, is the basic penetration step for singles, doubles, high crotches, and duck unders. You can lead with either leg. You take a big forward step with the lead foot and push off the trail foot **(2-2)**. Make sure you don't "wind up" by leaning back before you shoot in, since this telegraphs your shot. Your head should be up and your back straight. Keep your chest (and therefore your weight) over your lead leg. If your lead foot is too far in front of your chest you will be open for a pancake. If you can penetrate deep enough without hitting the mat with the knee of your trail leg, that's fine. Otherwise, hit down on that knee and bounce right up **(2-3).** Don't slide on that knee and don't go down to your other knee. The surest and easiest finishes to singles, doubles, and high crotches are from the standing position; so the penetration step should ideally get you in and right up, not just in (and then being stuck underneath the opponent on both knees). If you are practicing the penetration step by yourself, you should come back up to a good stance after each shot, and your elbows should be in close to your body throughout the whole move to prevent the man from underhooking you.

Figure 2-2

Figure 2-3

Lifting

No matter what position from which you're lifting a man: in front, behind, on the side, or down on the mat, lift with your legs, not your back. To do this, you must get your hips in tight to the man **(2-4)**. If you are doing it right, it should be no effort at all.

Figure 2-4

Bruce Kinseth lifting his opponent.

Hip Heist

This move can be used for an escape from almost all positions. The following description is from the referee's position, but whether the move is done from the referee's position, from a sit-out, a switch, or from a stand up at any level, the basic action is the same. You want to get as far away from the man as possible; so the first move is to take a big step with the outside foot at a 45° angle (2-5). This extends the top man and weakens his grip around your waist. Next, the inside leg is kicked forward just as in a long sit out (2-6), and while the inside leg is still in the *air,* the outside leg is kicked *straight* out (2-7). Before either leg hits, you should turn toward the *outside* by whipping your outside elbow down, (if he has his arm around your waist this elbow action will not only help you turn but will also free your waist), and throwing your inside leg over your outside leg. As a basic skill, this can be practiced without a man on top of you.

Figure 2-5

Figure 2-6

Figure 2-7

Back Arch

This movement is used in several throws, especially freestyle throws. The throw can be used from in front, back, or on the side of the man. The following description is for a position in front of the man. The hips are the key to the move. You must first get them in tight to the man, and then explode with them for power. To do the former, you must first step in between his feet with either one of your feet, and then step the other foot to the outside of his feet, therefore straddling one of his feet **(2-8)**. When stepping, you must bend your knees so your hips are *below* his. In most throw situations, both men have throw possibilities; so it's a combination of whoever has the best body position and takes the initiative that decides who throws and who gets thrown. Next, explode your hips into him and *arch* back **(2-9)**. This should send his legs flying in the air. Keep the arch through the entire move, look straight back over your head, land on top of your head **(2-10)**, and then turn **(2-11)**. Do *not* tuck your chin so you land on the back of your head. This takes away your arch and will hurt more. As you are arching back, bend your knees slightly forward to take some of the weight off your head.

This move can be practiced in four different stages: 1) Standing with your back about two feet from a wall and then arching back and walking down the wall with your hands, touching your head, then walking back up the wall **(2-12)**. Then, move six inches closer to the wall and repeat the above. 2) With a partner, grab his hand, step inside his feet with one foot, on the outside with the other, explode your hips in, arch back and have your partner control your descent and then pull you up after your head hits **(2-13)**. 3) Alone: Repeat all the key steps without a partner: step in, explode your hips, arch back, hit on top of your head and then turn to your base **(2-14)** 4) Drill on actual throw with a partner **(2-8 to 2-11)**.

Figure 2-8

Figure 2-9

Figure 2-10

Figure 2-11

Figure 2-12

Figure 2-13

Figure 2-14

Back Step

This is the basic movement for headlocks, hip tosses, arm and shoulder throws. Whichever foot you lead with, step across to the toes of his opposite foot. Don't step way past his foot, because this will extend you and take away your power. Then, step your other foot up so that the toes of that foot touch the outside heel of the lead foot and form an "L" **(2-15).** Your knees should be bent so that your hips are lower than his. When you actually throw the move, your feet might not be exactly in this position, but they should be close. Once you've formed the "L", you *don't* take any more steps. Rise up on the balls of both feet and pivot on them **(2-16).** You should end up with both your feet being parallel and pointing in the opposite direction **(2-17).** They shouldn't be any more than six to eight inches apart, and your knees should still be bent. Your hips should be *completely* through. This is the key to the move. If you led with your right foot, you should end up with your *left* hip outside his right hip. Once you've reached this position, you just have to straighten your legs to get his weight off his feet **(2-18),** and then finish the throw **(2-19).**

Figure 2-15

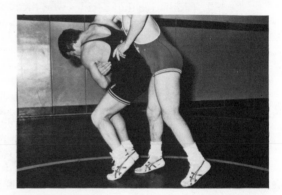

Figure 2-16

Figure 2-17

Figure 2-18

Figure 2-19

Coming to a Base

This is the *correct* way to get back up to your base after you have been broken down. Bring one knee up to your side **(2-20)**, then push *back over* that knee to your base **(2-21)**. The wrong way to come up is to do a push up **(2-22)**. Against a lot of wrestlers, you won't be able to get up at all this way. But even if you can, you have to use more energy than in the correct method plus the top man can easily put an arm bar in on you.

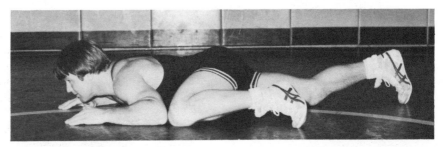

Figure 2-20

Figure 2-21

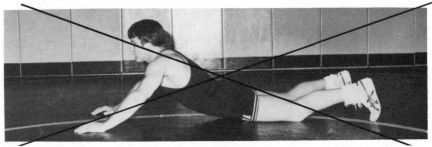

Figure 2-22

3
TAKEDOWNS

There is probably a greater variety in takedowns than in any other aspect of wrestling. Takedowns can be initiated from a variety of positions: without touching your opponent, from various tie-ups, as a second or third move in a chain of takedown attempts, or as a counter to your opponent's move. A takedown can attack an opponent's upper body, lower body, or both. Then, once a takedown has been initiated, there are numerous ways of finishing it. A successful wrestler is aware of these many options and automatically uses the right one, depending on the situation.

There is probably a greater variety in takedowns than in any other aspect of wrestling.

Double Legs

Penetration Step

You can lead with either your inside or outside foot. If you lead with your inside foot, step that foot between his legs as least as deep as his feet are **(3-1)**. Don't over-extend yourself, though. Your shoulders should always be over your lead knee as you shoot in. For further penetration, keep driving into your opponent and go down to the knee of your lead leg and step up your other foot to the outside of his foot **(3-2)**. Ideally, you will lift him or finish right away. There are finishes you can do when you get stuck underneath him, but it's usually best to spend the least amount of time possible on your knees. In fact, it's possible to get a double leg without hitting either knee. Once you are close to the other wrestler, bend your knees to lower your hips **(3-3)**, drive in with your head on either side and your shoulder in his gut, and grab behind both his knees **(3-4)**. Continue to drive into him and pull both of his feet off the mat **(3-5)**.

Figure 3-1

Figure 3-2

Figure 3-3

Figure 3-4

Figure 3-5

Figure 3-6. Lou Banach, in the finals of The NCAA's, illustrates the proper standing position for the double leg.

Finishes From Three Levels: Standing, Penetration Level, and On The Mat.

STANDING

Both of your arms are controlling his hips or thighs and you have his feet off the mat (3-6).

● **Turk** - this is one of the first finishes you should be considering, since it takes the man right to his back in a hold that's tough to get out of. You lift his near* leg so that you can step across him with your near leg and hook above his far knee (3-7). Drive through him, and as you hit the mat, land with your weight on him, your head slightly off to the side, and post your near arm so you don't roll through (3-8). You can then adjust by hooking his near shoulder and driving your elbow to his ear (3-9) or by throwing in a half-nelson (3-10).

● Swing both of his legs high to the same side your head is on to clear his legs (3-11). Step your inside knee in as you take him to the mat (3-12). The knee acts as a block in case you didn't clear his legs enough and he tries to get his inside leg down as a post. Finish with a half nelson.

*"Near" is used to describe his or your arm or leg that is on the same side as your head. "Far" refers to the side opposite your head.

Figure 3-7

Figure 3-8

Figure 3-9

Figure 3-10

Figure 3-11

Figure 3-12

● If you can't swing his legs high enough to prevent him from posting his inside leg, swing them as high as possible; then just as his legs are at this high point, change your arms so that you are hooked around his lower leg and are controlling his near lat **(3-13).** Drop down to your near knee, leaving the other knee up. Set his hip on your knee, keep control of his low leg, and put a half nelson on him with your other arm **(3-14).** All that's left is to take him to the mat. He still has an arm to post with, and even though you can probably drive him right over it, the finish is more effective if you eliminate his post by circling him towards the front as you take him to the mat **(3-15).**

● Taking the man over your head:

Your far arm is going to throw him over your head: to do so, drive that arm up hard from his hip to under his arm and keep on driving over your head. At the same time, duck your head to the outside (so he will slide off of it easier), pull down on his inside hip, and back slide-step with your near leg **(3-16).**

Figure 3-13

Figure 3-14

Figure 3-15

Figure 3-16

● Catch the elbow around your waist:

He will often reach around your waist. If he does so, trap his elbow if you can (if he's around your waist deep enough), but if you can't, grab his wrist **(3-17)**. You can just sit out with you near leg, arch back, and take him directly to his back **(3-18)**. Instead, you can come down on your near knee, swing his legs away from your head **(3-19)**, pivot on that knee as you turn your body in the same direction in which you moved his legs. Then pull down on the arm or elbow you have trapped, and arch over to his back **(3-20)**. As you arch back it's important to hold his arm *tightly* or else he'll end up on top of you. As he lands on his back, let go of his legs, but keep control of the arm or elbow across your chest. Your back will be on his chest, your body perpendicular to his **(3-21)**. You should be able to hold him there long enough to get three points; but if you can't or if you've already gotten your back points and can't pin him, step your high leg over toward his legs and come into his crotch with your arm.

Figure 3-17

Figure 3-18

Figure 3-19

Figure 3-20

Figure 3-21

PENETRATION LEVEL

You have control of his near leg, with your near arm around his thigh. Your far arm is controlling his far hip or waist **(3-22)**.

● **Turk** - The move from this position is the same as from the standing position.

● **Knee Sweep** - Pull his near leg to the outside so you can step your far leg to the outside of his far leg **(3-23)**. You will not step and plant your foot but instead sweep his knee in with yours (your leg will be bent and your knee will be sweeping just above his knee) **(3-24)**. When you pull his near leg to the outside and also lift it, his knee is easier to sweep. At the same time you sweep his knee, use your arm that is around his waist to pull him down in a circular motion. There are three key movements—lifting his near leg through the whole move, sweeping (your aim is to block and sweep, *not* hook and trip) his far knee, and pulling down his far side.

● **Ankle Sweep** - It's the same basic movement as the knee sweep, except instead of sweeping his leg with your knee, you are going to sweep his ankle with your foot. Again, you don't hook his leg with yours (it is *not* a trip). The sweeping leg should be straight. Also, lift his near leg and pull down and in a circular motion with your underhook, just as with the knee sweep **(3-25)**.

● **Trip Leg** - Use both arms to lift him and get his weight off his foot that's on the mat. At the same time, step your leg behind the inside of his far knee, **(3-26)** then drive your shoulder into his chest or stomach as you sweep his leg toward you and off the mat **(3-27)**.

● **Dump** - This move can be done with his leg between **(3-28)** or to the outside of your legs. You slide-step toward his leg that is on the mat (you take a short step toward that leg with your foot that is closest to it), **(3-29)**, and then take a big, backwards, and circular step with the other foot **(3-30)**. You should put pressure on him with your waist-control arm to help bring him to the mat. As with any finish, make sure he goes down to the mat before you do **(3-31)**.

● **Double leg tackle** - Push into him so he pushes back. When he does, you basically just tackle him by driving your shoulder into him as you pull his thighs together **(3-32)**.

● **Lift** - Lower your hips and step your inside leg in deep between his legs, so you get your hips under his **(3-33)**, then lift him. Once he's up in the air, use any of the finishes from that position explained earlier.

Figure 3-22

Figure 3-23

Figure 3-24

Figure 3-25

Figure 3-26

Figure 3-27

Figure 3-28

Figure 3-29

Figure 3-30

Figure 3-31

Figure 3-32

Figure 3-33

ON THE MAT

You are on both knees, your head to one side, and controlling the back of his thighs **(3-34)**. With each of these finishes, your knees have to be underneath your upper body (you can't be sprawled out). To get them underneath you, simply walk them up.

● **Hooking his leg** - If you lead with the inside leg, drive through the man so you go down on your inside knee. Then, step up with your outside foot, hook his leg and drive through him **(3-35)**. If you lead with your outside leg, you must step behind his foot and hook his leg as you drive through him, then finish as above.

● **Cutting his knee** - Chop the outside of his far knee with your far arm, and at the same time come up on your near foot and drive into him **(3-36)**. Use your head to help drive him over.

● **Duck under** - As you let go of his far thigh and change to a high crotch position **(3-37)**, throw your head back to help move his arm and body past you **(3-38)**. The move works best if you pull his legs into you and then do the duck under as he is trying to sprawl his hips back.

Figure 3-34

Figure 3-35

Figure 3-36

Figure 3-37

Figure 3-38

● **Taking him WITH your head** - Lift his feet off the mat or lift him enough so most of his weight is off his feet **(3-39)**. Pull down and in on his far leg, lift his near side leg still higher, and use your head to drive him to the mat **(3-40)**.

● **Taking him OVER your head** - This works best when he doesn't have both legs sprawled back equally but instead his near leg and knee are into you more than his far leg **(3-41)**. You use the same type movement you did when he was in the air and you took him over your head **(3-42)**, but down on the mat it is even more important that you throw your arm over your head hard and duck your head in the direction you are taking him because he's in a good position to wizzer you.

● **Catching his elbow around your waist.** If his legs are sprawled back you can hit the roll explained in the single leg section **(3-110 to 3-112)**, or, you can pull his legs into you and finish as explained in the standing position **(3-19 to 3-21)**.

Figure 3-39

Figure 3-40

Figure 3-41

Figure 3-42

Figure 3-43

● **Head between his legs** - If your head does get stuck between his legs, you can change to a single or else bring your knees up under you enough so you can lift him **(3-43)**. There are three finishes you can do from this position. You can release one of his thighs and use that arm to pop his knee up on that same side, while you pull down on his opposite knee. Turn your head toward the side you are pulling down to help his leg get over your head **(3-44)**. You can also throw the arm that you release over and around his opposite leg **(3-45)** and slide out behind him **(3-46)**. The third option starts just like the last move, then with the arm that was around the outside of that thigh, reach behind your back as you turn your upper body towards the leg you are controlling **(3-47)**. Bring that arm around his waist **(3-48)**, and pull him over your head **(3-49)**. Keep control of his leg and waist and drive him up towards his shoulders **(3-50)**.

Figure 3-44

Figure 3-45

Figure 3-46

Figure 3-47

Figure 3-48

Figure 3-49

Figure 3-50

Counters to Double Legs

Just as against a single leg, you want to square your hips **(3-51)**. You may initially counter with a wizzer, but after that square your hips to him. His head will usually be to the outside; so you can usually cross face him and spin around the other way **(3-52)**. Whether his head is to the outside or between your legs, if you are having trouble getting your legs free, reach behind his arm, lock palm to palm around his chest, arch your hips into him and pull up on his chest at the same time **(3-53)**. This should free your legs. If he shoots in with his arms out **(3-54)**, he's open for a pancake **(3-55)**.

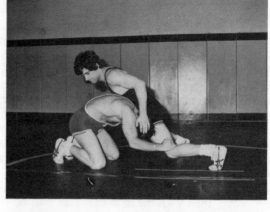

Figure 3-51

Figure 3-52

Figure 3-53

Figure 3-54

Figure 3-55

Single Legs

There are three basic types of single legs:

- ● High leg single
- ● Low leg single
- ● Snatch single

High Single Leg

LOCKING HANDS

Grip your hands together palm-to-palm with your *outside hand on top* **(3-56)**. The other wrestler will only be able to grab your inside wrist, and if he tries to pull it up to break your grip, he will be pulling it straight into your other hand. He should *not* be able to break your grip. However, if you grab his leg with your inside hand on top **(3-57)**, the only thing keeping him from pulling your hands apart will be the fingertips of your outside hand. He can easily break this grip.

POSITION

● Lock your hands behind his knee - not above or below it.

● Put your forehead in his ribs, *not* on his thigh.

● Be on your toes, able to move.

● If he gets your head down, **(3-58)**, throw your inside shoulder into him **(3-59)**, circle your head away and then back into his ribs **(3-60)**.

Figure 3-56

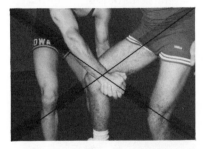

Figure 3-57. Wrong technique.

Figure 3-58

Figure 3-59

Figure 3-60

PENETRATION STEP

● Step with your outside foot **(3-61)**.

● Lead with your inside arm to prevent the wizzer. He can only wizzer your outside arm, so if you lead with it, he will be able to sprawl and wizzer your arm before you have a chance to get a good grip on his leg **(3-62)**. If you lead with your inside arm, he won't have a chance to wizzer you until after you have solid control of his leg **(3-63)**.

FINISHES FROM THREE POSITIONS

Finish #1: His leg between yours.

● **Dump -** From a good single leg position **(3-58)**, drive your outside shoulder into him so that he has to take a step forward on his other foot. After driving your shoulder into him, your bicep and outside shoulder should be on his thigh **(3-64)**. Take a short *backward* step with your outside foot and at the same time put *shoulder* (not head) pressure down on his thigh **(3-65)**. *Don't* go down to the mat with him until after he is down.

Figure 3-61

Figure 3-62

Figure 3-63

Figure 3-64

Figure 3-65

● Pinch his leg between yours, reach behind your butt, and grab his foot **(3-66)**; then dump him as above.

● **Block his opposite knee in front or back -** Use your front arm when blocking the back **(3-67)**, use your back arm when blocking the front of his knee **(3-68)**. Use shoulder pressure and circle (behind when doing the front block, in front when doing the back knee block), to bring him down. If his foot that is on the mat is pointing out, he is hard to dump but is open for the knee block. If his foot is pointing in, the opposite is true. Therefore, use one move to set the other one up. *Chain* your moves together.

● **Change to a double -** Pull the man toward you so he has to hop his foot toward you. As he hops toward you, drive into him and step your back foot behind his far foot; then change to a double and drive him down **(3-69)**.

Figure 3-66

Figure 3-67

Figure 3-68

Figure 3-69

● **Sit back** - This finish works best when the other wrestler has his weight forward, and especially if he has a wizzer and is driving you forward. Unlock your hands and slide your outside hand up to his crotch **(3-70)**. Next, step your inside foot across to his far foot, sit down on your inside hip, and use your head to drive his chest or stomach back **(3-71)**. As soon as you hit, come up on top of him **(3-72)**.

● **Hooking and lifting his leg** - From the good single leg position described above **(3-58)**, hook his leg (that you are holding) with your outside leg **(3-73)**; then drive into him with your head still in his ribs, post your arms out to the side for balance when you hit, and lift his leg through the whole move **(3-74)**. If he pushes your head to the outside, hook his leg with your inside leg and drive into him with your shoulder **(3-75)**. Finish as above.

Figure 3-70

Figure 3-71

Figure 3-72

Figure 3-73

Figure 3-74

Figure 3-75

● **Stepping your inside leg behind his leg** - This can be done in two ways: If you are in a good single leg position, step your inside leg out and back, while at the same time lifting his leg **(3-76)**. As soon as your leg is behind his leg, step it in and underneath his leg and set his leg on your inside hip **(3-77)**. Your leg should move in a continuous movement: out, back, and then in and under his leg.

Figure 3-76

From a good single leg position, or if he has your head down, you can get into the same position a second way. Pinch the lower part of his leg between yours to help hold his leg. Then unlock your hands and reach down between your legs to his heel with your inside hand **(3-78)**. After your have control of his heel, step your inside leg out, back, and then back under his leg. At the same time you lift his leg so that when you step your leg back under his, his leg is up on your hip **(3-79)**. The forearm of your inside arm should be tight to your chest to trap his foot so that he won't be able to kick free. From here, the following five finishes can be used:

Figure 3-77

1) **Trip forward** - With your leg that is nearest to him, trip *above* his knee and drive him forward **(3-80)**.

2) **Trip backward** - This is actually more of a block than a trip. You circle towards the front so that he has to hop backward to keep his balance. At the same time you step, block his ankle with your foot so that he can't move it **(3-81)**. Before you circle, you can also switch your hand that is around his knee to an underhook. Then, when you circle and block, pull down on his shoulder **(3-82)**.

Figure 3-78

Figure 3-79

Figure 3-80

Figure 3-81

Figure 3-82

3) **Knee pressure** - Switch your hand from under to over his knee. Grab just above his knee, then twist and pull down his leg while your other arm keeps his ankle from turning **(3-83)**. You can also slide step towards his other foot, just as in a dump, to help take him to the mat.

4) **Tree top** - This move can be done two ways. The first is as a continuation of clearing his leg to the inside **(3-76 to 3-77)**. Instead of lifting his leg just enough to get it on your hip, you can lift it as high as you can so his other foot comes off the mat. The second way is from the knee and heel control. Again, just lift it as high as possible, but also take a big step away from him **(3-84)**. This extends him and makes it easier to get him off the mat **(3-85)**.

All four of the aforementioned finishes can also be done when both of your arms are underneath his leg. To get into this position, (once you've reached the knee and heel position), use your knee to lift and hold his leg up **(3-86),** while you change your hand from over his ankle to under it **(3-87)**. It's important to use your knee, because if you try to hold his leg just with your other arm while you switch from over to under his ankle, he can easily power his leg down to the mat. With both arms under his leg, you can raise his leg even higher; but it has the disadvantage that he can turn away and kick free easier since you don't have his heel trapped as well as in the other position. There is one more finish from this position that can't be done from the knee and heel position:

5) **Cradle** - Lift his leg high so it gets near his head. Some men will lean forward, bringing their head even closer to their knee. If they do, change your arm that is under his knee to around his head, and at the same time slide the other arm up under his knee and lock up the cradle **(3-88)**. Circle him backwards down to the mat then.

Figure 3-83

Figure 3-84

Figure 3-85

Figure 3-86

Figure 3-87

Figure 3-88

Figure 3-89

You can get into this position in two ways: You can put his leg outside or he can do it. Some men will put their foot to the outside, but keep their knee inside to block you. Simply lift his leg up onto your hip; then if his knee is still on the inside, you can just hit it out with your inside arm and then relock your hands **(3-89).** If he keeps his leg inside yours **(3-90)** and you want it outside, clear it the same way described above for clearing his leg to the inside, except this time you will be stepping your *outside* leg out and then back in **(3-91 to 3-92).** When his leg is to the outside of yours, you can change to a double by clearing his leg even farther to the outside so you can step in and reach around his waist with your inside arm **(3-93).** From this position, any of the finishes described for the double from the penetration level can be used.

Without changing to a double, the following finishes could be used:

● **Dump** - Do it just as you did when his leg was on the inside.

Figure 3-90

Figure 3-91

Figure 3-92

Figure 3-93

● **Barsagar** - Lift his leg up and step across towards his other foot. Both of these actions, lifting and stepping, will cause his weight to shift over his other foot so that unless he steps it out, he will fall down. Once you've stepped and lifted his leg onto your hip, release your inside hand and *block,* don't chop, his opposite knee so he can't step with that leg **(3-94).** Continue to lift his knee through the whole move **(3-95).** When the move is finished he should be on the mat but you should still be on your feet. Cover him *after* he is on the mat; don't go down with him.

● **Heave-ho** - Put pressure in on his knee to get him to react and push it out. When he does, throw his leg out and up as high as you can, stepping your same side leg out somewhat at the same time so his other leg doesn't hit it on its way up **(3-96).** You should bring his other leg completely off the mat so he goes down to the mat **(3-97).**

● **Heave-ho to a turk** - If you can't get his leg up high enough to get his other leg off the mat **(3-98),** you should have cleared it enough so you can step into a turk **(3-99),** just as explained above.

Figure 3-94

Figure 3-95

Figure 3-96

Figure 3-97

Figure 3-98

Figure 3-99

Figure 3-100

● **Head chop** - Slide step in front towards his other foot and at the same time release your inside arm and "club" the side of his head with your forearm and drive him down to the mat. At the same time that you slide step, you can also block the inside of his ankle with your outside foot **(3-100)**. This move can also be done with his leg to the inside.

● **Blocking in front of his far ankle** - If you can't get him down with the head chop, hook your hand around his head, slide step toward the back, block the front of his ankle and pull his head down **(3-101)**. The head chop can be used to set this move up and vice versa; or with your hands still locked around his knee, you can slide step toward the back, block the front on his ankle, and put pressure on his knee to take him down **(3-102)**.

● **Dropping underneath him** - If he's pushing down on your head **(3-103)**, drop down to your inside knee, post your inside arm, lift his leg, and drive your head underneath it **(3-104)**. From here, turn to the outside and come behind him **(3-105)**. Another option you have when he is driving your head down is to grab his heel, turn your head away from him, and then lift his leg so you finish with the heel and knee control described above **(3-79)**.

Figure 3-101

Figure 3-102

Figure 3-103

Figure 3-104

Figure 3-105

Finish #3: His leg is on the mat.

● Control his leg with your outside *arm* (not hand) across the back of his knee **(3-106).** Post with your inside arm, raise your shoulders and bring your knees up underneath you, and then straighten your back to lift him further **(3-107).** Finish with any of the options when your head is between his legs on a double **(3-43 to 3-50).**

● Post both hands, your outside hand on top of the inside one, raise your butt up, drive your shoulder into his thigh, and then run behind him **(3-108).** He will usually come up with you so you end up in a standing single leg position.

● When spinning around behind him, if you can put your back forearm and elbow down on the mat on the inside of his leg; **(3-109),** he won't be able to turn and follow you. You can then just spin behind him and finish the move.

● Roll - If he reaches around your waist on the outside, grab it with your opposite side arm **(3-110),** sit your legs under to the inside, pull his arm tight and lift your head to throw him over **(3-111).** You should be able to hold him there long enough to get back points **(3-112),** then "high-leg-over" and turn toward his legs.

Figure 3-106

Figure 3-107

Figure 3-108

Figure 3-109

Figure 3-110

Figure 3-111

Figure 3-112

Low Leg Single

Use the same penetration step as for the high leg single, but reach below his knee **(3-113)**. Again, lead with your inside arm and bring your outside arm around his leg after you get in. Ideally you post your hands, spin, and come right around him **(3-114)**. (You should shoot in *straight* and then spin. *Don't* shoot off to the side as you penetrate.) If you get stopped down there **(3-115)**, the possible finishes are:

● Spin around (turn-the-corner) to the back and pick up his ankle.

● Turn-the-corner, grab above his knee, and drive your shoulder into his thigh to get him sprawled forward **(3-116)**.

● Always be looking for his other ankle. If you turn the corner and he leaves it close enough, grab it and drive over it **(3-117)**.

● **Blocking his knee.** With your back arm reach across to the front of his opposite knee or ankle and trip him forward **(3-118)**.

● **Hyper-extend his lower leg.** When you are in front of him, grab his heel and pull it toward you while you drive in with your shoulder at his knee **(3-119)**.

Figure 3-113

Figure 3-114

Figure 3-115

Figure 3-116

Figure 3-117

Figure 3-118

Figure 3-119

Snatch Single Leg

When doing any of the snatch single legs, you grab behind his *knee* with just your fingertips **(3-120)**. You're not shooting in on him, only stepping; so you won't be able to get in deep enough to grab him any better. You will easily be able to lift his leg off the mat because the different set-ups will shift his weight off the leg you are going to snatch. Once you have his leg up, either drive into him or run backwards with it (on your toes, not your heels) so he is off balance. Pinch his leg between your knees as you move him so you can adjust your hands to the proper grip **(3-121)**. If you try to stay still for even a short time with just your fingers holding his leg, he will drive his leg down to the mat and free it. It's a continuous movement - you are moving him as soon as you snatch his leg so he has to hop on his other leg, taking all the weight and pressure off his leg that you are holding.

Figure 3-120

THREE DIFFERENT SNATCH SINGLES

● **Change levels** - If you're close enough all you have to do is change levels, (bend you knees and drop your hips), and snatch his lead knee **(3-122)**.

● Use one arm to hit (or push) the man's shoulder hard enough so he has to step back with his other leg for balance and in so doing takes all his weight off his other foot; (if you do it slowly and easily, he will step back his same side foot, but if you do it hard with your arm stiff, he will step back his opposite leg - this is what you want). At the same time, reach across behind the knee **(3-123)**. You should be able to lift it with just one hand, then bring down your other arm and lock your hands the right way as you pinch his lower leg between your knees.

● From head and arm control **(3-124)**, snap his head and his arm to the opposite side on which you are controlling his arm. Your elbow of the arm that is controlling his head stays almost stationary - it acts as a pivot as you rotate his head down and then out with your hand **(3-125)**. This should turn his body and make him step his far leg to you. Snatch it with the hand that was around his head (as soon as you finish throwing his head by, bring that hand back in the opposite direction to catch his leg as he steps it by) **(3-126)** and then lock your hands.

Figure 3-121

Figure 3-122

Figure 3-123

Figure 3-124

Figure 3-125

Figure 3-126

Set-ups

Whatever set-up you use, it should do two things: bring his leg close enough to reach easily and clear his arms. You can make him put his leg where you want by moving him, such as circling *away* from the leg you want to shoot for, or you can fake one move and rely on his reaction to open himself up. Besides circling the man, the different movement setups are:

● **Pop** - If his arm is on your shoulder or he is reaching for you, pop up his arm(s), *above* the elbow (so he can't just bend his arms up) **(3-127)**.

● **Chop** - Same positions as applied to the pop but chop his arms down. If he's anchored solidly on your shoulder, move back quickly just before you chop to loosen his grip **(3-128)**.

● **Drag** - Reach across with your opposite arm and grab him *above* the elbow **(3-289)**. You don't want to drag him by you, but just open up his side so you can shoot in on him **(3-292)**.

● **Shrug** - If he has his arm on your head or shoulder, reach across with the opposite hand and grab his wrist. Grab his head or tricep with your other arm **(3-129)**. Throw your shoulder into him to get his arm loose, push his arm across his body and then shoot in on his leg **(3-130)**. You can also shrug him from an underhook **(3-224)**.

● **Snap** - Snap his head down, then when he reacts and pulls it up, shoot in. As you shoot, you may have to pop his arms up to clear them.

● **Block** - From inside control you can just raise his arm out of the way **(3-131)**. With no control, you can shoot in and block his arms out as you penetrate **(3-132)**.

SET-UPS FROM FAKE SHOTS

● **Fake to one leg and shoot in on the other one.** Just take a quarter step toward the one leg **(3-133)**, enough to get him to step that leg back and leave the other one out for you to shoot in on **(3-134)**.

● From an underhook, step your hips in, as if going for an ankle pick, then when he squares in front of you single or high crotch him **(3-228)**.

● Fake drag to one side and shoot in on the other side.

● Go for any of the snatch singles to one side. If you miss it, it's usually because he stepped his leg back and left the other one out. Then the opposite side should be open for a single or high crotch.

Figure 3-127

Figure 3-128

Figure 3-129

Figure 3-130

Figure 3-131

Figure 3-132

Figure 3-133

Figure 3-134

Counters to Singles

You always want to square your hips to the man **(3-135)**. You might turn your hips and counter with a wizzer as he shoots in on a high single, but after you've sprawled back you then square your hips. Your wizzer then becomes an overhook on the side where he has your leg. From here, there is a series of moves you can use:

● **1/4 Nelson** - Put your free hand on his head, drive it down to the mat, then grab your own wrist with your wizzer arm **(3-136)**. From here, push down on his head, pry up on his arm, and take him to his back **(3-137)**. Instead of pushing down on his head, you can also grab his chin with that arm **(3-138)**. Again, grab your own forearm or wrist, and pry him over to his back.

● **Head lock or pancake** - Push down on his head with the 1/4 Nelson, then when he reacts by driving it up, let him come up with it, release your hand from his head, and use that arm either to hit a headlock **(3-139)** or come under his far arm and hit a pancake **(3-140)**. As you head lock or pancake him, use your overhook arm to pull his arm forward and therefore extend him further **(3-141)**.

Figure 3-135

Figure 3-136

Figure 3-137

Figure 3-138

Figure 3-139

Figure 3-140

Figure 3-141

● If you're sprawled back far and can reach under both his arms with your wizzer arm and grab his far wrist **(3-142)**, pull it off your leg, keep control of it, and then spin around that side (since he can't reach that arm out to stop you) **(3-143)**. If he is deep underneath you, reach behind both his arms and grab his far upper arm **(3-144)** and finish just as if you had his wrist. If you grab his far arm and he is still holding onto your leg, sprawl back as far as you can to get him stretched out, walk toward the side on which he has your leg **(3-145)**, (keep pulling his far arm so his head is down), then step your legs over his back **(3-146)**. Since he still has a hold of your leg, you will pull him right to his back **(3-147)**. You can also reach in front of his arms with your other arm and grab his far upper arm with that arm too **(3-148)**. Pull his arm with both of your arms and at the same time step your knee up to block his shoulder on that side. Pull him right over that shoulder onto his back **(3-149)**.

Figure 3-142

Figure 3-143

Figure 3-144

Figure 3-145

Figure 3-146

Figure 3-147

Figure 3-148

Figure 3-149

● If you have the wizzer on and he steps over your near leg **(3-150)**, lift that leg up **(3-151)**, pull down with the wizzer, and pull down on his far arm if you can reach it **(3-152)**.

● If he tries to step all the way over your back, raise your butt up and **(3-153)** pull down with the wizzer **(3-154)**.

● If he comes up to his feet while you still have the wizzer on, you can use it as a set-up for the fireman's carry **(3-282 to 3-283)**.

There is also a series of counters when he's on his knees that don't involve using a wizzer:

● **His head to the outside** - Cross face and grab his opposite upper arm **(3-155)**. Circle away from his head, back toward his feet. If you can't break his grip, reach back with your hand and try to pull his hand off your leg. When you get back near his legs you can scoop his near leg with your inside leg **(3-156)** or else you can put your head into his side and reach for his ankle with your back arm **(3-157)**. Once you have his ankle turn it out, since that will turn his upper body away from you, allowing you to go completely behind him.

Figure 3-150

Figure 3-151

Figure 3-152

Figure 3-153

Figure 3-154

Figure 3-155

Figure 3-156

Figure 3-157

● **Setting him on his hip** - Square your hips to the man and reach back and grab the inside of his near ankle **(3-158)**. Lift and pull his ankle out so you set him on his opposite hip **(3-159)**. From here you just circle around to his feet.

● **Turning the inside hip down** - Walk your leg back as far as you can. If you can't break his grip, arch your hips into him, putting even more pressure on his arms, then turn your hip down, driving his shoulder down to the mat **(3-160)**. This should break his grip, and you can just spin around that side.

● **Blocking his head** - Described in the section on freestyle turns **(6-1 to 6-7)**.

● **Cobra** - If he lifts up his knee, reach under it **(3-161)** and pull his knee tight into your chest so his head is trapped **(3-162)**. Once his head is trapped, sit on your hip (of the leg he is holding), straighten that leg, and reach for his other leg with it. Hook it **(3-163)**, then roll him back to his back **(3-164)**. This can also be done when he is on his feet.

● **He pulls your leg up tight** - Grab his far lat and his near arm, then step your leg across to block his opposite leg **(3-165)**. Pull up on his arm, down on his leg, and lift his knee with your leg as you drive over him.

If the man comes up to his feet with your leg, there are also several moves you can use from there:

● **Basic Defense** - One of the basic things you almost always want to do is get his head down. Push his head down with your hands **(3-166)** and then cover it with your hips to hold it down **(3-167)**. He now has to use his lower back to hold you up, so he is using a lot more energy than you are. With your inside hand you can grab his inside hand. This stops him from doing the barsagar, the head chop, changing to a double, etc. Therefore by holding his head down and controlling his inside wrist, you limit his mobility, make him use a lot more energy, and take away a lot of his offense.

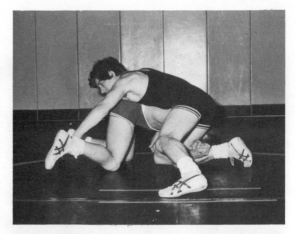

Figure 3-158

Figure 3-159

Figure 3-160

Figure 3-161

Figure 3-162

Figure 3-163

Figure 3-164

Figure 3-165

Figure 3-166

Figure 3-167

● **Trip him back** - After you have gotten his head down, hook your leg through the inside and then behind his leg **(3-168)**. Reach behind his other knee with your hand, then hip into him and drive him to his butt **(3-169)**.

● **Ankle Pick** - Have your foot to the outside of his leg and have your knee above his. Grab the upper part of his far arm; then hop backwards and pull that arm toward you **(3-170)**. This causes him to step his free leg toward you. After one of his steps, release his arm and reach down to his ankle, drive your weight into him at the same time, and also kick into him with your knee, driving him over that ankle **(3-171)**.

● **Leg blocks** - After you have gotten his head down, drive your leg down to the mat and to the outside of his ankle, blocking it. Cross face and grab his opposite arm above the elbow. Reach over his back and under his far arm and grab your wrist with your other arm **(3-172)**. Lift that arm and pull him over your foot **(3-173)**. Or, with your hands locked the same way, you can step inside his near leg or all the way across to the outside of his far leg **(3-174)**, drive your weight forward, and lift his leg with yours **(3-175)**.

● **Trip back** - Your leg is in between his. *Straighten* your leg and hook your foot behind his far knee. Have a wizzer in and hop backwards so you get to the side of him. Lower your hips, reach behind his near knee with your free hand, **(3-176)** and take him backwards **(3-177)**. By keeping straight the leg he is holding, you pry on his legs - out on his far one and in on his near one. If you bend your leg you lose this pressure. You can finish by cradling with your leg still across him **(3-178)** or else by scissoring your legs out and getting perpendicular to him.

Figure 3-168

Figure 3-169

Figure 3-170

Figure 3-171

Figure 3-172

Figure 3-173

Figure 3-174

Figure 3-175

Figure 3-176

Figure 3-177

Figure 3-178

● **Knee tilt** - After you have got his head down, reach behind the outside of his far knee **(3-179).** Pull him into you first, locking his head, then bend your knees and lift him right over your leg that he has a hold of **(3-180).** *Don't* sit on your butt and roll him back. Post your free hand behind you, then lift him over your leg and finish on top of him **(3-181).** This move can also be done if he is on his knees on a single and he brings his knee up.

● **Sag throw** - If he has his hands locked wrong, (inside instead of outside hand on top), wizzer his near side, grab his inside wrist with your other hand, and stamp your foot down to the mat **(3-182),** on the outside of his leg, breaking his grip. At the same time underhook his far side **(3-183),** and you are in position for the sag throw described later **(3-405 to 3-408).** If his hands are locked the right way around your leg, it usually is not possible to break his grip.

● **Kickout** - Lift your knee up a few inches so it is *above* his hands. Then, straighten your foot and kick your leg out by driving your knee down toward the mat **(3-184).** When your leg is free turn to face him.

● **His head is to the outside (3-185)** - Whether he puts his head to the outside or you put it there, you have to watch out for him changing to a double. However, with his head to the outside, there are several things you can do:

a) **Circle behind** - Block his inside arm (so he can't change to a double) and circle behind him **(3-186).**

b) **Arm drag** - hook inside his arm **(3-187),** then hit an arm drag, turning your hips as you go down so he lands flat and you land on top of him or on your inside hip **(3-188).**

c) **Switch** - reach over his inside arm and under his same side leg **(3-189),** then hit a switch **(3-190).**

Figure 3-179

Figure 3-180

Figure 3-181

Figure 3-182

Figure 3-183

Figure 3-184

Figure 3-185

Figure 3-186

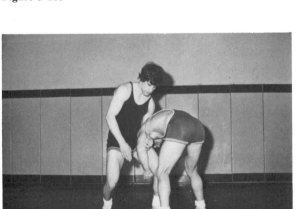

Figure 3-187

Figure 3-188

Figure 3-189

Figure 3-190

COUNTERS TO A LOW LEG SINGLE

When a man is behind you on a low single, you want to hold his head down and back with your inside hand so he can't come up and reach above your knee **(3-191)**. From here, you can do a couple of different things:

● Plant your other foot on the mat where you will be able to push off it but he can't reach it. Point the toes of the foot he has straight back so it will come out easier. Push back into him first and then pull your leg out hard. At the same time reach your outside arm back to his *far* hip so you can turn in a tight circle **(3-192)**. Once your foot is free, pivot on your planted foot and spin behind him **(3-193)**.

● Make sure you have his head planted on the mat, then step your free leg over his back **(3-194)**. As soon as you have stepped to his other side, lock around his far leg with both your hands so they are up in his crotch **(3-195)**. Use your leg as a block and lift him right over it and onto his back **(3-196)**.

Figure 3-191

Figure 3-192

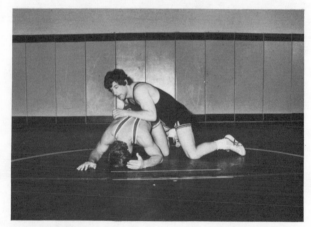

Figure 3-193

Figure 3-194

Figure 3-195

Figure 3-196

High Crotch

Penetration Step

Step with your outside foot and go down to your inside knee. Turn your outside shoulder back so you could look at your back foot if you wanted to. Whether you are controlling his arm, elbow, or wrist: you throw it *back* over you. Throw your inside arm high up into his crotch. Keep your shoulder and head tight to his side **(3-197)**. If he's leaning into you or if you throw his arm back hard enough, he will often go down with this initial shot **(3-198)**. If he doesn't, you can use one of the following finishes:

Finishes

● **Change to a double** - His hips should be square to you to do this. As soon as you hit on your inside knee you should use your outside foot to drive across him. The arm that was controlling his arm comes down and controls the outside of his thigh, and the other arm goes across to control his opposite thigh. As you bring it across, you should be bringing your inside foot up and stepping across to the outside of his legs **(3-199)**. It's an explosive move—you are on your knee only for an instant—you hit on it and then bring it up. To make sure your arm doesn't get caught as you change to a double, keep it in tight as you reach for the other leg. You then use any of the double leg finishes.

● **Single leg finish** - If he's straight onto you, you can finish with a single or double, but if he is turning the corners on you **(3-200)**, a single is your best, if not your only, option. You drive into him and come up to both feet, just as with the double leg finish. However, if he has an angle on you, you won't be able to get the double; so just come up with the single **(3-201)**. Your head will be on the outside when you finish; so you should readjust your head so it's in his ribs.

Figure 3-197

Figure 3-198

Figure 3-199

Figure 3-200

Figure 3-201

FINISHES IF YOU GET STUCK ON THE MAT
WITH BOTH KNEES DOWN

Your inside hand will be up high and through his crotch while your outside arm will be across his knee **(3-202)**. He will usually counter you by putting most of his weight down on his leg you have and holding your inside arm in so you can't reach across and change to a double **(3-203)**. If he isn't sprawled back too much and your hips are fairly tight to him you can:

● Pull his leg in tight to your chest, come up on your outside foot, and then lift him by first straightening your back and then arching it backwards **(3-204)**. Your hips must be in tight. As you lift him, swing your inside foot to the outside and pivot on your inside knee **(3-205)**. He should fall in front of you as you spin around the back of him.

● If you can lift him some but not enough to finish the move as just explained, you should have made him forget about blocking your inside arm enough so that you can change to a double **(3-199)**.

● Again, come up on the outside foot, only this time start driving straight across his other foot and over your inside knee **(3-206)**. This shifts his weight to his other leg and makes it hard for him to keep blocking your arm. When you feel as if you're going to fall over your knee, step that leg up and all the way across to the outside of his far leg so you are blocking it. As you are stepping you should be changing to a double **(3-207)**.

Figure 3-202

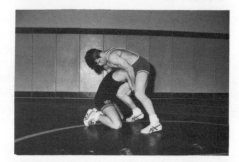

Figure 3-203

Figure 3-204

Figure 3-205

Figure 3-206

Figure 3-207

● If he reaches around your waist with either arm, grab it with your outside arm (that was around his knee) **(3-208),** then lift him as high as you can, arch back, and finish just as you did when he reached around your waist when you were in on a double. **(3-19 to 3-21).**

● Change from controlling his crotch to controlling his knee **(3-209).** Drive your shoulder into his thigh as you pull his leg out and set him on his butt **(3-210).** Finish by circling towards his legs **(3-211).**

If he is sprawling back and your hips are too far out to lift him:

● Try to walk your hips up underneath him by stepping up first with one knee and then the other.

● As he tries to sprawl back, drop your *inside* arm from up his crotch to across his knee and hook your hand on his shin **(3-212).** With this control, when he sprawls back his leg will come off the mat **(3-213).** You just have to pivot on your inside knee and spin around him **(3-214).** If you try to control him with your outside arm, his leg will just sprawl back rather than lifting up **(3-215).**

● If he is sprawled back slightly but you can still reach his foot, reach around the outside of the bottom of his foot and control his heel **(3-216).** (If he's sprawled back he will be on his toes and his heels will be up.) Turn his foot out **(3-217),** and this should turn his body away from you so you can just come up behind him.

Figure 3-208

Figure 3-209

Figure 3-210

Figure 3-211

Figure 3-212

Figure 3-213

Figure 3-214

Figure 3-215

Figure 3-216

Figure 3-217

Tie-ups and Set-ups

● **Elbow control** - He has his hand on your shoulder and you are pinching his elbow with your palm up and thumb to the outside **(3-218).** Your other arm should be free to reach through his crotch. Throw his arm out **(3-219)** and then *back* over you, duck your head just enough to let it under his arm; then snap your head back to help throw his arm and body past you **(3-197).** If the thumb of his hand that is on your shoulder is to the outside, you should have no problem doing the move. If his thumb is to the inside and he is holding your shoulder, you might need to use your other hand to come across and hit his forearm to knock his arm off your shoulder. The rest of the move is the same.

● **Inside control (3-220)** - The only problem of throwing the high crotch from inside control is that after you throw his arm back you might have a problem bringing your arm back forward without his underhooking it. To avoid this, you should "reach for your gun": After you have snapped his arm back, keep circling your arm behing you and then bring it forward fast and tight to your thigh **(3-221),** just as if you were reaching for your gun.

● **Controlling his wrist or he's controlling yours** - Just as from inside control, you must "reach for your gun" to clear your arm.

● **Underhook** - Use your underhook or else hip into him so that he squares his hips to you **(3-228).** When he does, hit the high crotch just as explained above.

Figure 3-218

Figure 3-219

Figure 3-220

Figure 3-221

Underhook Offense

Whenever you have an underhook, make sure you are controlling him, rather than allowing him to control you. He has an overhook; so if you're not lifting his arm with your underhook he can control you. If he does control your arm, he has excellent control to throw a fireman's, so your other arm should either be right in front of you so you can block with it or else control his other wrist **(3-222)**. Some opponents will wrestle with their arms out, and it is easy to underhook them. Other wrestlers keep their elbows in. In order to underhook such a wrestler, you have to grab around his head with your other arm and jerk his head away from the side you want to underhook **(3-223)**. This will bring his elbow out so you can underhook him. There are a number of moves you can do from the underhook control.

● **Shrug** - If his arm is very limp, throw it over your head as you duck your head, reach your other arm across his waist, and step in with your inside knee to block him from running through **(3-224)**.

● **Ankle pick** - Step your inside hip in front of him and with that hip plus your inside leg raise his near leg so all his weight is on his other foot **(3-225)**. Pull down on the underhook so his head is below yours. When you bring your leg back down to the mat, bring it down just to the outside of his far ankle to block it **(3-226)**. By using your ankle as a block, you can usually drive him over it and not even have to grab his ankle with your hand. To make sure he doesn't step over it, though, you should reach down for the ankle with your free arm. All through the move, your weight is over his far ankle—you never lean back, but drive right over his blocked ankle, use your underhook to drive his head towards his knee.

Figure 3-222

Figure 3-223

Figure 3-224

Figure 3-225

Figure 3-226

● **Leg snatch** - If his arm is too tight to shrug and get completely behind him, throw it up as far as possible to clear his near leg and at the same time reach down with your free arm and grab his leg at the inside of his knee **(3-227).** As soon as you have his arm as high as you can get it, drop your underhook arm straight down and lock with your other hand.

● **Single or high crotch** - Step your hip in as if you are going to throw him or ankle pick him. If he leaves his other leg close, ankle pick him. He will usually try to square in front of you, though. When he does, his near leg is open for a single or high crotch **(3-228).** Whichever you hit, throw his arm up and over you with your underhook.

● **Drag** - With the underhook, pull him straight down toward your inside foot **(3-229).** When you've pulled down to about your stomach, or waist level, bring your other arm, palm up, over and down on his arm, above his elbow **(3-230),** clearing it so he can't grab you. Step your inside foot back so he doesn't fall into it. The underhook arm pulls him down, your other arm clears his arm and finishes the move. As you bring that arm down over his, pull out your underhook so it doesn't get caught.

● **Barsagar** - Circle away from his opposite leg so he will step it towards you. Just as he steps it, block the outside of his knee with your free hand and drive him over it **(3-231).** Keep the underhook, but change to controlling around his back and use it to help drive him over his knee. He won't always go down right away, but keep driving right over his knee and eventually he will fall **(3-232).**

● **Double leg** - Again, you have to hip into him or jerk the underhook to get him to face you. As he is facing you, (not after he already has and is in a good defensive position) step into the double, leading with either your inside or outside leg, and with your head on his side opposite the side you had underhooked **(3-233).** If you put your head on the same side as your underhook he can turn the corner on you easier.

Figure 3-227

Figure 3-228

Figure 3-229

Figure 3-230

Figure 3-231

Figure 3-232

Figure 3-233

Seat Belt

The seat belt is the position where your arm is around his back and your arm is controlling his far hip (**3-234**). You can drop into this from an underhook, or else after you have shot in on a single leg you can change your arm from around his leg to around his back as you come up with it. From the feet you can:

● **Bear hug** - As he tries to face you, step in front of him and lock up the bear hug, catching his arm if possible **(see p. 87).**

● **Hip toss** - The move is best if you can grab his wrist as you throw him, but it works even if you don't have it. You simply do a backstep to his far foot, making sure you get your hips all the way through (**3-235**).

● **Throw** - Put your free hand on his opposite side chest or shoulder. Step your foot that's on the same side as your free hand over to his far foot so that your hips are in tight to him (**3-236**). From here, do a back arch, exploding your hips in, pushing on his shoulder, and pulling back on his hip (**3-237**). As illustrated, the same throw can also be done with an overhook.

When you start hipping in for the hip toss, he will often go down to his knees. It's important to keep tight control of his hip. There is also a series of moves from here:

● If his head is down, reach over the top of it (**3-238**), put your fist into his chest, then *circle* him down towards the front (**3-239**).

● If you start to rise to go over his head and he comes up with you (**3-240**), you can often just pull his hip back and take him over backwards (**3-241**).

● If he comes up with you and reaches for your far arm (**3-242**), bear hug him, with or without his arm trapped (**3-243**).

Figure 3-234

Figure 3-235

Figure 3-236

Figure 3-237

Figure 3-238

Figure 3-239

Figure 3-240

Figure 3-241

Figure 3-242

Figure 3-243

Duck Unders

The penetration step for duck unders is the same as with high crotches—you step with your outside foot, hit on your inside knee, and come up immediately. Just as with the high crotch, throw his arm *back* over you, not just out. Also, don't duck your head a foot under his arm. Just duck it enough to get it under his arm, and then use your head to snap his arm back **(3-244)**. There are several different tie-ups from which the move can be done:

● **Head and arm control** - Pull his head down to one side as you duck under his arm on the opposite side **(3-245)**.

● **Lat and arm control** - From an underhook, control his lat, then pull down on it as you duck under his opposite side.

● **Inside control of both sides** - You can pull one of his elbows in **(3-246),** then when he reacts by pushing it out, throw it out and back as you duck it. Or, you can fake to one side, then hit the duck on the other side.

● **Wrist control** - Either you have his wrists or he has yours. Whichever happens to be the case, you can either hit the move directly to one side or else fake one way and go the other.

● **Underhook or seatbelt control** - (Your arm is around his back and controlling his far hip **[3-234]**.) You can grab his wrist or he can grab yours.

Figure 3-244

Figure 3-245

Figure 3-246

● **Head lock position** - With your hands locked, fake a headlock toward the side on which you have his arm trapped **(3-247)**; then when he reacts hit a duck under on that side **(3-248)**. When locked up for a headlock like this, though, he can also duck under you if you don't have him tight enough **(3-249 to 3-250)**.

● **Head control and he reaches** - When you get head control the other man will often reach up to control your head or shoulder. *As* he reaches (not after he has control of your head) you should hit his arm up above his elbow and duck under him.

There is also more than one way to finish each of the duck unders:

● Keep control of his head or arm on the opposite side you are ducking and bring him down to the mat **(3-251)**.

● Bring the arm, (that threw his arm back), behind him and in his crotch, drop the other arm to around his waist and control his far hip, then lift him **(3-252)**.

● After you hit on your knee, bounce up and come completely behind him **(3-253)**. Do *not* leave your arm that was on his other side completely across his chest or stomach or he'll roll you **(3-254)**.

● **Bear Hug** - After you've got your head under his arm **(3-255)**, bring your inside leg across to the outside of his far leg so you are blocking it. At the same time, bear hug him with your arms, trapping his far arm if possible **(3-256)**. Once locked up, take him over the leg you have blocked.

Figure 3-247

Figure 3-248

Figure 3-249

Figure 3-250

Figure 3-251

Figure 3-252

Figure 3-253

Figure 3-254

Figure 3-255

Figure 3-256

Fireman's Carry and Near Arm Far Leg

Fireman's Carry

You can lead with your inside or outside leg, but in all of the different carries the most important part of the move is to pull your opponent's shoulder down tight to yours and hold his arm tight. When you first penetrate, you throw his arm out so you can get your head underneath his arm. Once it's under, though, pull his arm down tight so his shoulder is next to yours, and pinch his lower arm next to your side with your elbow. Another point common to all of the finishes is that you release his leg as you finish the throw so your arm doesn't get caught. Also, keep control of his arm even when you finish the move, since you should be able to hold him on his back.

Mike De Anna in on a fireman's carry.

STEPPING WITH YOUR INSIDE LEG FIRST

● With all fireman's carries your head is going to the outside of his legs. There are two finishes if you step with your inside leg first **(3-257).** With the first, you go down on your outside knee **(3-258),** pivot on that knee as you turn towards it, then go down on that same side shoulder and throw his leg over **(3-259).**

● The second option is to lead with the inside foot but to turn perpendicular to him and land on both knees **(3-260).** You then lift his crotch and pull down on his arm to take him to the mat. If hit explosively, you don't even have to go to your shoulder.

Figure 3-257

Figure 3-258

Figure 3-259

Figure 3-260

STEPPING WITH YOUR OUTSIDE LEG FIRST
(3-261)

● Again, there are two options. The first is to take a long step with your inside leg between his legs **(3-262)**, go down to your shoulder, and throw his legs over **(3-263)**. This is the *worst* of the finishes, though, since this gives the other man his best chance of stepping over your legs and then holding you on your back **(3-264)**.

● **Driving straight through:** In this finish, you don't hit and then turn, but keep your momentum going and drive straight through him. You can either drop your outside knee right behind his leg **(3-265)** and then drive him over it **(3-266 to 3-267)** (you should finish in a straight line) or just drive straight through him (drive straight over and down on your outside knee, and throw him off in front of you).

Figure 3-261

Figure 3-262

Figure 3-263

Figure 3-264

Figure 3-265

Figure 3-266

Figure 3-267

HE PULLS HIS ARM FREE

If you're in tight on his leg but he pulls his arm out, just come around the outside of his knee and you're in the high crotch position. You can intentionally let his arm go, if you like, finishing with the high crotch better than with the fireman's.

YOU KEEP CONTROL OF HIS ARM BUT HE SPRAWLS THE LEG BACK AND YOU LOSE IT

There are two options if you keep control of his arm but he sprawls his leg back and you lose it:

● Bring your free arm across to the outside of the leg you originally controlled. Block his knee with your palm (thumb down) **(3-268),** pull his arm down, drive into him, and pry up on the knee **(3-269).**

● Bring your free arm up around his waist on the opposite side **(3-270).** Pull down on his arm and throw your arm up hard **(3-271).**

Figure 3-268

Figure 3-269

Figure 3-270

Figure 3-271

YOUR HEAD GETS CAUGHT

If you finish the fireman's but you can't get your head out **(3-272)**, there are a couple of things you can do:

● Keep a hold on his arm and his leg, and drive him up toward his shoulders **(3-273 to 3-274)**. You might pin him this way, but usually when he gets this close he releases your head and tries to get to his stomach.

● You can flip straight across him **(3-275 to 3-276)**, then turn toward his legs **(3-277)**.

Figure 3-272

Figure 3-273

Figure 3-274

Figure 3-275

Figure 3-276

Figure 3-277

Near Arm Far Leg

Again, the key point is to keep his arm tight. In this move, instead of controlling his arm on the same side as the leg you are going to attack, you attack the leg on the opposite side on which you are controlling his arm. You must not only keep his arm tight, but pull it down with you as you attack his opposite leg. If you keep it tight, you should turn his shoulders to the mat when you shoot in on his leg. You control his leg at the thigh or knee, and can put your head to the inside **(3-278)** or outside **(3-279)** of his far leg. You have to drive farther to put your head on the outside, but if you keep his arm tight it turns his shoulders more. To finish, you go down to your shoulder and throw his leg over **(2-280).** The move is typically done with inside control, but it can also be done from the over-under hook position described later. **(3-418 and 3-419).**

SET-UPS FOR THE FIREMAN'S AND NEAR ARM FAR LEG

For either move, you should have the man stepping into you. In addition, you should clear his free arm so you can penetrate to his legs. Some set-ups that work for both are:

● **Control his arm.** Push his opposite shoulder back with your other arm enough to make him step back with his far leg **(3-281).** While the far leg is back and his near leg is still close, it is a good time to throw the fireman's. When he brings the far leg back into you, it is a good time to throw the near arm far leg.

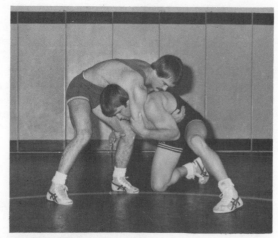

Figure 3-278

Figure 3-279

Figure 3-280

Figure 3-281

● **Pull down on his head.** You can also pull his head down so he reacts by pulling it up and throw either move, since he will clear both his legs when he pulls up. It's best if you can get him stepping into you too, and you should also pop his other arm out of the way with your free arm, if he is blocking you with it.

● **Wizzer.** This is an excellent way to get him squaring up to you. Wizzer him hard so he has to bring his far leg around to keep from being thrown **(3-282)**. It also gets his legs fairly wide apart so it is easy to come into the fireman's carry. When you throw the move, you change from an overhook to controlling his upper arm **(3-283)**.

● **2-on-1.** Just as with the wizzer, you can get him squaring up to you with his legs far apart. Just throw your shoulder into him **(3-377)**.

● **Fake one, go for the other.** Controlling his arm and reaching for either move is a good set-up for the other since he will usually step back the leg for which you are reaching and leave the other one out to attack.

● **Front head lock.** From a front head lock **(3-284)**, circle him toward the side you have his arm trapped on. Then, keep control of his head with your one arm, drop your shoulders underneath him and reach up his crotch with your other arm **(3-285)** and finish just like any fireman's **(3-286)**. Keep his arm trapped to the side of his head throughout the move.

● **Drag.** After you have cleared his arm across the front of him **(3-287)**, keep control of his arm and throw a fireman's to the opposite side **(3-288)**.

Figure 3-282

Figure 3-283

Figure 3-284

Figure 3-285

Figure 3-286

Figure 3-287

Figure 3-288

Arm Drags

In all of the different drags, you use both of your arms for different things. One is a guide arm - it just starts to move his arm in the right direction. The other arm is the power arm - it hooks his arm and moves it the rest of the way **(3-289).** You can go down to your inside hip and scissors his leg **(3-290),** but he can step over you **(3-291).** It's a lot safer to use the drag to clear his side **(3-292)** (by turning him slightly and moving his arm across) so you can shoot in on either a double or single. After you have cleared his arm, you can also step your leg across and hook around the back of his leg **(3-293).** Drive into him with your chest, and as you take him down, put both hands out to the side so that you don't get rolled when you hit **(3-294).** There are various set-ups that you can use:

Figure 3-289

Figure 3-290

Figure 3-291

Figure 3-292

Figure 3-293

Figure 3-294

● **You have inside control. (3-295)** Release his upper arm and rotate your hand and forearm to the outside of his forearm, keeping your elbow in the same place **(3-296).** Once your forearm is to the outside of his arm, bring it down and back so that you start to drive his arm to the inside. Your guide arm therefore goes in a complete circle—up, out, down, then back in. At the same time, your other arm comes across and *hooks* (rather than grabs) his arm above the elbow **(3-297).** Your power arm then pulls his arm across the front of him, clearing his side so you can shoot in **(3-298).** This same drag works as he is reaching for your head or shoulder, or when he already has control of either one of them.

● **You have his wrist.** The hand and arm that is controlling his wrist is your guide arm. You start to move his arm across with that arm and at the same time come across with your other arm, *hook* above his elbow, and finish just as before.

● **He has your wrist.** Everything's the same as when you have his wrist except that in order to clear your wrist you may have to slap it across and hit your opposite side hip. This should break or at least loosen his grip so that you can finish the drag as described above.

● **Redrag.** When he starts to drag you and hooks your arm with his power arm **(3-299),** you can hook his arm and drag him **(3-300).**

● **Drag from an underhook.** This set-up is described in the underhook section **(3-229 to 3-230).**

Figure 3-295

Figure 3-296

Figure 3-297

Figure 3-298

Figure 3-299

Figure 3-300

Ankle Picks

● **From an underhook.** explained in the section on underhooks **(3-225 to 3-226).**

● **Controlling his head. (3-301)** Circle away from his far leg, so he steps it toward you. Stop circling, then drive his head toward his ankle just as he steps it **(3-302).** Keep your head *above* his, otherwise he can shuck you. Grab the outside of his ankle and drive over it **(3-303).** If he steps that foot back as you reach for it **(3-304),** drive back toward his other ankle and pick it **(3-305).**

● **From a front headlock.** Explained in the section on front head locks **(3-366).**

● **From down on the mat.** If you have stopped one of his takedown attempts down on the mat and then he steps his foot up close enough for you to grab it **(3-306),** drive his head and his weight over it **(3-307).**

Figure 3-301

Figure 3-302

Figure 3-303

Figure 3-304

Figure 3-305

Figure 3-306

Figure 3-307

Bear Hugs

When locking up a bear hug, it's best if you can get one of his arms trapped, but the move is effective even if you don't have an arm trapped. As you step into a bear hug, your head is going to be on the same side as his arm that you have trapped. If you don't trap an arm, it doesn't matter what side your head is on, but you always step in between his legs with your leg that's on the side opposite your head **(3-308).** You lock your hands palm-to-palm, just as in a single leg.

Figure 3-308

Ed Banach bear hugging his opponent.

Bruce Kinseth bear hugs his opponent.

Finishes

● Step your other leg up next to the outside of his leg (**3-309**). Use your leg as a block and take him back at a 45° angle (**3-310**). You will either land on your shoulder or else with him on his back (**3-311**).

● After you have stepped your outside leg up to block, use it to push his knee in and at the same time squeeze your inside knee between your other knee and his leg so that both your legs are outside his (**3-312**). Then just take him backwards (**3-313**).

● **Hip throw.** Lower your hips below his and step in your leg (the one that's on the side opposite your head), pull him tight to you so you stay chest-to-chest; then take him to his back (**3-314**).

● **Crunch him.** This is easiest to do when you're under both of his arms. Your hands should be locked around his lower back (**3-315**). Use your arms to pull his back in, and at the same time use your shoulder and/or head to drive into his chest. You should be able to bend him straight back (**3-316**).

● **Leg trip.** Hook his leg from the *inside,* then drive into him as you lift the leg (**3-317 to 3-318**).

Figure 3-309

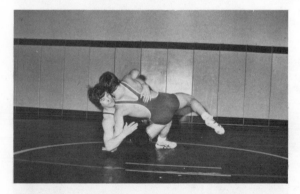

Figure 3-310

Figure 3-311

Figure 3-312

Figure 3-313

Figure 3-314

Figure 3-315

Figure 3-316

Figure 3-317

Figure 3-318

Set-ups

● **From a single or double leg shot.** After you've shot you can slide up his leg to around his back with your outside arm, and at the same time release your other arm, step in with your leg (the one on the same side as your arm that's around his back), drive your head to his other side, and lock his arm on that side. This move works best when he's trying to face you.

● **Pummelling.** As you are pummelling, if you can get inside control on both sides, lock it up. If you can't, just as you change your hand (you pummel inside with one and he does the same on the other side so you are over one arm and under the other), step in with your leg (that's on your underhook side) with your head to your overhook side and lock your arms up, trapping his arm.

● If you're standing behind him with control, you can bait him to wizzer you and turn into you. When he does, step in with your head to his far side and lock it up.

Counters

● **Head lock.** If you can sag your hips back enough to give you room to get your hips through, hit a head lock.

● **Fake headlock, block opposite leg.** After faking a headlock, he will usually shift his weight in the opposite direction. As he does, do the following three things at the same time: grab the back of his neck and pull his head to that side, step your leg to the outside of his far leg so you are blocking it, and reach your arm into his crotch **(3-319)**. From here, lift and pull him over your knee.

● **Hip toss.** From an over-under hook, you can set up a hip toss by straightening up slightly, baiting him to step in for a bear hug. As he steps in, he is moving to your side, so it makes it easier for you to get your hips through. Make sure you lower your hips below his **(3-402 to 3-404)**.

● **Hook your foot in.** Hook your foot inside his leg. If you can get your arm underneath his far arm, it will help you to throw him. Either wait for him to throw you or else you can initiate the throw by hopping your free leg across his far foot, then arch back, keeping your foot hooked until after you've hit the mat **(3-412 to 3-417)**.

● **Front Sal to.** When he's straight in front of you and under both arms, over hook both your arms, put your fists into his chest; try to bring your elbows in to break his grip, then step in and hit a back arch **(2-8 to 2-11)**.

● **Push his chin away.** Put both hands under his chin and drive it up, sagging your hips back at the same time **(3-320)**.

Figure 3-319

Figure 3-320

Short Offense

The short offense is a series of moves you can use when both you and the other man are on your knees facing each other. You usually get into this position when he has shot on you and you stop him before he gets to your legs or vice versa. You may end up in a variety of positions:

● One of the best ways to counter his shot is to block his collar bone with your forearm and block his upper arm with your other hand. As he shoots in, you can often snap his head to the mat and spin around him, but often you end up controlling the back of his head with the hand that blocked his collarbone and controlling the tricep on his other side with your other arm **(3-321).** From here, a number of moves can be done:

HEAD SNAP RUN AROUND

From the head-and-arm control position, drive into him, using your forearm on his collar bone to drive his weight back and get his hands off the mat so he doesn't have a four-point base **(3-322).** Then he will usually push back into you. As he does, use both hands to snap his head down to the mat where your knee *was* **(3-323).** (Your knee won't be there since as you start to snap him down you should also start spinning around him **(3-324).**) As you spin around him, first your arm that was on his arm blocks his arm so he can't reach it out to catch you; then as you get farther around, the arm that was controlling his head blocks the arm.

Figure 3-321

Figure 3-322

Figure 3-323

Figure 3-324

SHUCK

Use your forearm to snap his head (and therefore his body) away from you. At the same time, use your other arm to pull him that way **(3-325).** You just need to turn his body a little and then spin around to the side you cleared. One good time to hit this move is right after he has shot in and you stop him on his knees. Another good time is after you have tried to snap his head down and he pops it back up. You can also use the head shuck as a set-up for the head snap. If you shuck him but don't turn him enough to get around him, snap him down as he brings his head back.

HEEL PICK

If he steps either foot way up, grap his ankle **(3-326)** and drive his head over it **(3-327).**

HEAD LOCK

Drive into him just as at the start of a head snap to get his weight shifted back. Then throw your arm that was controlling his head way past his head, as if you were trying to punch somebody two feet behind him, so his head ends up in your arm pit **(3-328).** At the same time, use your other hand to pull his arm on the other side *forward.* (You don't want to headlock him straight over his knee that is acting as a brace, but rather toward the front where he has no brace.) As you drive into him, you will be off the knee and on your foot on the side toward which you are headlocking him, and as you finish, that knee stays up and you sag down to your other hip **(3-329).**

The move can also be set up with a 1/4 nelson. **(3-139)**

● Instead of blocking his forearm and controlling his head, you can also counter his shot by underhooking one side, (usually the side he shot to), and controlling his arm on the other side. You end up with his head under your chest. You should be off your knees so he can't grab them and so you have more weight on him **(3-330).** From here, you can:

Figure 3-325

Figure 3-326

Figure 3-327

Figure 3-328

Figure 3-329

Figure 3-330

PANCAKE

Just as in the headlock, you don't want to drive him over his knee sideways, but instead pull him forward **(3-331 to 3-332)**. This extends him, gets him off his base, and helps clear his head. The last of these is important. If his head stays under your arm when you pancake him, you might not be able to hold him because a good man will just spin through. If you use your chest to move his head to the side of your chest opposite that on which you have the underhook, it becomes easier to pull his head up as you pull his arm forward. If you try the pancake but only drive him down to his shoulder or elbow **(3-333)**, you can pull your underhook arm out and spin around the side his shoulder is down on, using your other arm to block his arm **(3-334)**.

HEEL PICK

Just as explained previously **(3-326 to 3-327)**.

BARSAGAR

If he comes up off his far knee but doesn't step up enough so you can heel pick him, grab the outside of his knee, come up on both feet **(3-335)**, and run and drive him over that knee **(3-336)**. You don't try to chop the knee, but just block it so he can't step with it. You can often bait him into coming up with that foot by taking some of your chest weight off him as if you are going to come to your feet.

Figure 3-331

Figure 3-332

Figure 3-333

Figure 3-334

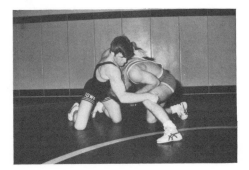

Figure 3-335

Figure 3-336

KNEE TAP

Reach across with your underhook arm to the outside of his opposite knee or just above it. The palm of your hand should be against his knee with your thumb down **(3-337)**. Come up on your feet and drive straight into him over that knee. If you can, drive him all the way to his side or back **(3-338)**, use the arm that blocked his knee to come under his arm so you can keep him on his back. Your other arm should be controlling his other arm throughout the move. If you only knock him down flat **(3-339)**, use the arm that is controlling his arm to block that arm, and then spin around that side as he tries to come back up to his base.

SHUCK

Come up on your toes and start running him in a circle away from the underhook side. Then, "unhook" your underhook arm so your forearm is along the side of his face or his neck **(3-340)**, and shuck him in the same direction in which he is already moving **(3-341)**.

OTHER MOVES

There are other series of moves that can be included in the short offense, such as the front headlock **(3-342 to 3-364)** and 1/4 nelson **(3-136 to 3-141)**, covered elsewhere.

Figure 3-337

Figure 3-338

Figure 3-339

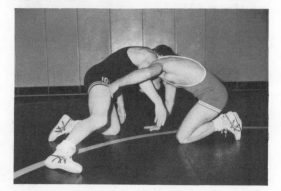

Figure 3-340

Figure 3-341

Front Head Lock

Down on the Mat

POSITION (3-342 to 3-343)

Whether you have the front head lock on when he is on his feet or down on his knees, you should be over his head with one arm and around the outside of the upper part of his far arm with your other arm. Your forearm should be across his face and turning his chin away. Your elbow of that arm should be up high so he can't reach it with his far arm **(3-344)** and short drag it **(3-345 to 3-346).** Your other arm should be pulling his arm forward and have it tight to his head. You can either lock your hands, palm-to-palm, or else keep them unlocked and control his head and arm separately. You should be on your toes, your head should be in his arm pit on the side where you have his arm locked, and your shoulder on the other side should be on top of his shoulders.

GETTING INTO IT

● If he shot on your legs and you countered with a wizzer, square you hips, keep the wizzer in as an overhook, then come over his head with your other arm and lock it up.

● If you countered his shot with an underhook, use your chest to drive his head to the mat. Your underhook can then become the arm around his head, and you can reach around his other arm with your other arm, then lock it up. Or, once his head is down, bring your other arm around his head and take your underhook arm out and reach around his arm with it.

Figure 3-342

Figure 3-343

Figure 3-344

Figure 3-345

Figure 3-346

FINISHES

● **Shuck.** Start running around toward his trapped arm (he has no post or block on that side.) Run hard, since he should not be able to follow you if he's just on his knees. Just go around him if you can. If you can't, use your forearm that is across his face to throw him by in the same direction you are running him **(3-347).** Your legs have to be back and you have to shuck him hard so he doesn't catch you with his free arm. If he's resisting really hard instead of trying to run around with you, you can shuck him back in the opposite direction **(3-348).**

● **Knee tap.** Use the arm that is around his head to reach across and block his knee **(3-349).** If you hit it hard enough, he will go over to his back **(3-350).**

● **Knee tap, spin around.** If you knee tap him but instead of going to his back he only goes flat **(3-351),** use your arm that is around his arm to block it and spin around that side **(3-352).**

Figure 3-347

Figure 3-348

Figure 3-349

Figure 3-350

Figure 3-351

Figure 3-352

● **Near side cradle.** Again, circle toward his trapped arm. He will often bring his knee up, trying to face you **(3-353).** If he does and you can get close enough to it, keep control of his head but with your other arm reach behind his knee. Put your head in his side to help fold him up so you can lock your hands **(3-354).** Finish using any of the near leg cradle finishes **(5-71 to 5-86).**

● Again, start circling toward the arm you have trapped. Use your outside arm to reach for his near ankle and put your head into his side so he can't grab your leg **(3-355).** With the hand that is around his head, grab his chin and pull it up and out. Once you have his ankle, pull it out. He will usually just go flat here and let you run around him. If he does bring his knee up, cradle him.

● **Roll thru.** This is a good freestyle move but can be used in high school too. You must have him locked up tight. Your head should be on the side of the arm you have locked. Set your near leg under your far leg **(3-356)** and as you roll through bridge on your head **(3-357)** (if you don't you'll lose points in freestyle). You can just come back to your initial position or you can scissor your legs as you are coming out of the roll and come up on top of him **(3-358 to 3-359).**

Figure 3-353

Figure 3-354

Figure 3-355

Figure 3-356

Figure 3-357

Figure 3-358

Figure 3-359

● **Pancake or headlock.** If he's really fighting to get his head up, let go with your arm that is around his head, then let him raise his head and use your now-free arm to hit a pancake (come under his arm), or a headlock. With your other arm keep control of his arm through the whole move.

● **Block his arm with your leg.** Step your opposite side foot up so your knee is blocking his arm that you have trapped **(3-360)**. Release your arm on that side and spin around him **(3-361)**.

● **Head Chancery.** Push his elbow in to make him react by pushing it out. When he does, pull it out, shoot your head underneath that arm, and keep your arm around his head **(3-362)**. Pull down on his head, lift up with yours; then grab and lift the outside of his leg **(3-363)**. He will end up on his back and you can finish with a cradle **(3-364)** or a half nelson.

Front head lock from the feet

You still have your hands locked the same way they were when you were down on the mat **(3-365)**. If he wrestles with his head down, you can just snap him down enough so you can put it on directly. Be careful of reaching too much, since you will open that side up for a duck or any type of leg shot. If you have an underhook, you can snap him down with that and reach over his head with your other arm. Then change from an underhook to locking around his arm. Once locked up, you can sprawl your legs back, bring him down to the mat, and use any of the finishes just covered, or from up on your feet you can:

● **Fireman's carry.** Explained in the section on fireman's carries **(3-284 to 3-286)**.

● **Ankle Pick.** Circle him towards the arm you have trapped so that he has to keep stepping his far leg toward you in order to face you. Just as he steps it, drive his head down toward it and grab his ankle **(3-366)**. Continue to drive him straight over his ankle and down to the mat.

Figure 3-360

Figure 3-361

Figure 3-362

Figure 3-363

Figure 3-364

Figure 3-365

Figure 3-366

2-on-1

To get into the 2-on-1: when he ties up with your head, grab his wrist with your opposite hand, turn your head away from the side he has hooked, then shrug your shoulder into him to help clear his arm and at the same time pull his wrist off your head (3-367). Hook your other arm under his armpit and grab the top of his bicep (3-368). Move the hand that did have his wrist to a point over his elbow and control the back of it with your hand (3-369). Twist his elbow and bicep in opposite directions—his elbow up and his bicep down. Keep your shoulder above his and keep weight down on his shoulder.

Finishes:

● **Drag near side.** If you can get far enough to the side you are controlling, simply drag his elbow by, reach your upper arm around his back, and step your front knee across in front of him so he can't run by you (3-370).

● **Single.** All you do is drop down to his leg on the same side you have controlled. Don't let go of the 2-on-1 and then drop, but take it down with you (3-371) and then snatch his leg so he can't block you (3-372).

● **Double.** If he puts his hand on your head or on your shoulder (3-373), drive up the arm you are controlling so it hits his other arm *above* his elbow and drive it up too, clearing his legs (3-374). If you hit his other arm below his elbow, he can just bend his arm and you won't drive his arm up. Don't release his arm until you have stepped in with your inside leg and with your head to the outside (3-375). You can also hit a double leg by just throwing his arms by, as in the drag described above. Most men won't let you get all the way behind them, but all you need to do is clear your opponent's side for an instant, then shoot in with your head on the same side as the arm you control. You don't have to go down to your knee; just step in, since you will already be in close to him (3-376).

Figure 3-367

Figure 3-368

Figure 3-369

Figure 3-370

Figure 3-371

Figure 3-372

Figure 3-373

Figure 3-374

Figure 3-375

Figure 3-376

● **Bear Hug.** Same move as the double, but go to his waist rather than to a double.

● **Fireman's.** He should be squared off in front of you to throw this. If he isn't, drive your shoulder into his shoulder and he should square up to you **(3-377)**. When he does, release the arm controlling his elbow and reach to the inside of his near leg and finish like any fireman's **(3-378)**.

● **Fireman's with just the arm.** Change your inside arm from controlling his elbow to controlling his wrist, and turn it down so his palm is facing you (this locks his arm **(3-379)**. Then, keeping his arm controlled by both arms through the whole throw, step into the fireman's position **(3-380)** and finish by driving through at about a 45° angle **(3-381)**. *Don't* turn after you get in and try to finish by taking him at a 90° angle to the direction you shot in, since he is likely to sag back onto you. As with all fireman's carries, it is very important to pull his arm down tight so his shoulder is tight to yours.

● **Ankle sweep.** Step across the front of him towards his outside leg. This will cause him to step forward with his near leg. As you step, straighten your inside leg out and block his inside ankle with your foot **(3-382)**. Block and lift his leg and pull down with the 2-on-1 **(3-383)**.

Figure 3-377

Figure 3-378

Figure 3-379

Figure 3-380

Figure 3-381

Figure 3-382

Figure 3-383

Lou Banach executes the Over-Under Hook.

Over-Under Hook

You have an overhook on one side and an underhook on the other side **(3-384).** Your head and most of your weight should be over your overhook side since that's his underhook side, and if he does lift you he will be lifting that side. He has the same tie-up that you have, so he can also do any of the following moves to you:

● **Under-arm spin.** It's best to get him pushing into you. The foot on your underhook side is going to step between and past your other leg and his leg. At the same time, throw your underhook arm hard up under his opposite arm **(3-385).** Your arm should hook his at your bicep. As you arch straight back towards his opposite knee, make sure you have his arm tight. Pinch it to your body with your overhook arm **(3-386).** On your way back turn away from his body and land on your knees and elbows, still controlling his arm **(3-387).** You should be blocking both of his legs with your body and be tight to them. Don't go flat—you won't be able to block him. As you hit, continue to roll through, pulling him over you **(3-388).** When you finish, get into the habit of pulling your inside arm out and reaching across his body **(3-389).** If you throw the move but end up to his side rather than directly in front of him **(3-390),** keep the arm tight, turn your head back and down towards your inside knee **(3-391),** roll to your hip and pull him over **(3-392).** You can really get a lot of pressure on his shoulder.

Figure 3-384

Figure 3-385

Figure 3-386

Figure 3-387

Figure 3-388

Figure 3-389

Figure 3-390

Figure 3-391

Figure 3-392

● **Knee block.** Circle towards your underhook side so he is stepping his other leg toward you. Just as he steps that leg, reach your underhook arm across to the outside of his knee. Turn your hand thumb-down so your palm is against his knee and will act as a block **(3-393).** When he starts to go down, pull out your arm that was blocking his knee **(3-394 to 3-395)** and *don't* go down to the mat until he is down. If you keep your arm in and go to the mat with him he can easily lateral drop you **(3-396 to 3-397).** The same move can also be done using your overhook arm to block his far knee **(3-398).**

● If he straightens his back so you can lock your hands, bear hug him, trapping his arm you have overhooked.

Figure 3-393

Figure 3-394

Figure 3-395

Figure 3-396

Figure 3-397

Figure 3-398

Figure 3-399

● **Tripping him over his opposite knee.** Circle toward your overhook side so he is bringing his opposite leg toward you. As he steps it up, step your underhook-side foot to the outside of his foot so that your knee is blocking his knee. At the same time that you step, reach your overhook arm across and into his crotch **(3-399).** You pull down with your underhook arm, lift his crotch, and pull him over your knee **(3-400 to 3-401).** You don't drive him backwards but sideways over your knee.

● **Hip toss.** Like most throws, the key to the hip toss is getting both of your hips through. It's best to get him circling toward your underhook side first and then do your backstep in the opposite direction. By moving him in one direction and then backstepping in the opposite direction, it helps you to get your hips all the way through. When you backstep in, have your knees bent so your hips are under his **(3-402).** Once both your hips are through and you're ready to throw him, straighten your knees so his feet will come off the mat **(3-403).** You pull down with your overhook and lift with your overhook to finish the throw **(3-404).**

Figure 3-400

● **Sag throw.** Step your leg that's on the same side as your overhook up next to his same side leg **(3-405).** Your leg should be blocking his leg, and your hips should be lower than his as you step in (otherwise he can hip toss you). It's best if you can lock your hands, but you don't need to. From this position, you just fall down to your shoulder **(3-406 to 3-407)** and then turn on top of him **(3-408).**

Figure 3-401

Figure 3-402

Figure 3-403

Figure 3-404

Figure 3-405

Figure 3-406

Figure 3-407

Figure 3-408

Ed Banach executing the hip toss to the other side.

● **Hip toss to the other side.** If his leg (that's on the side of your overhook), is sagged back and his other hip is up close **(3-409),** it's hard to hit the hip toss described above or the sag throw just described. He's open for another move, though, and that is to hip in with your overhook-side hip. Once again, have your hip below his, but from this position you won't be able to get your hips all the way **(3-410).** You can still finish the move, though, and it helps if you pull his chest tight to yours so that his back is twisted toward the mat **(3-411).**

Figure 3-409

Figure 3-410

Figure 3-411

● **Toe-in throw.** As with the sag throw, this can be done whether your hands are locked up or not. Hook your overhook side foot inside his calf **(3-412)** and step your other foot up close to him so your hips are tight with his **(3-413)**. From here you arch back, twisting toward your overhook side and lifting his leg through the move **(3-414)**. Even after you hit on your shoulder **(3-415)**, your foot should still be hooked and lifting his leg until you finish on top of him **(3-416 to 3-417)**.

● **"Near arm" far leg.** Your underhook control can take the place of arm control and you can drop to his leg on your overhook side **(3-418)**, pull down on his leg, and bring him down **(3-419)**.

● **Drop to a single.** You can just drop down to a single on the side you have overhooked. You can't simply reach down since he has an underhook on that side. You have to drop all your weight straight down **(3-420)** in order to penetrate his underhook **(3-421)**.

Figure 3-412

Figure 3-413

Figure 3-414

Figure 3-415

Figure 3-416

Figure 3-417

Figure 3-418

Figure 3-419

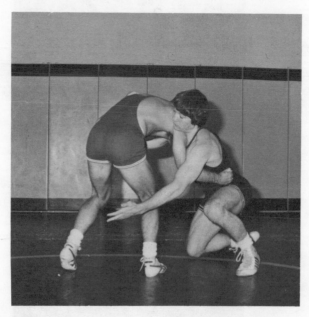

Figure 3-420

Figure 3-421

Headlocks

Just as with the hip toss, the most important part of the throw is getting your hips through. To get them through, pull him in one direction and then back-step in the opposite direction with your knees bent. When your hips are through and you're ready to throw him, that's when you straighten your legs so his feet come off the mat.

Set ups and tie ups

● **Head and arm control. (3-422)** Circle him toward the side on which you have head control **(3-423)**. Backstep and throw your arm way past his head so it ends up in your armpit **(3-424)**. Straighten your legs **(3-425)** and pull down on his arm to finish the throw **(3-426)**.

Figure 3-422

Figure 3-423

Figure 3-424

Figure 3-425

Figure 3-426

● **He ties up with your shoulder.** Reach over his arm and grab the inside of his elbow. Use your forearm to pinch his elbow to your chest **(3-427)**. Control his head with your other arm and finish just like the last head lock **(3-428)**.

● **Locked around his arm and head.** You can get into this position two ways: From a bear hug position, when you are over one arm, under the other, and locked around his back, slide both arms up so you are around his head with his arm pinched to the side of it. You should be able to finish the throw in the same movement. Or, from an underhook, reach around his head and lock your hands. You should stand him up straight and raise the arm you have trapped so it is along the side of his head **(3-429)**. From here you can:

Figure 3-427

Figure 3-428

Figure 3-429

HEADLOCK

Jerk him first away from the side on which you have his arm trapped **(3-430)**; then when he reacts, back step in and throw the headlock toward the side on which you are locked **(3-431)**.

HEADLOCK AND BLOCK

From the locked position, step your leg across to block his opposite leg above his knee **(3-432)**. As you step your leg, have all your weight driving over his leg. After you've blocked his knee, continue driving over him and lift his leg at the same time **(3-433)**.

Figure 3-430

Figure 3-431

Figure 3-432

Figure 3-433

Randy Lewis performing a headlock and block.

Figure 3-434

BLOCK THE OTHER WAY

If he steps his hip back on the side where you have his arm locked, and steps his other hip in to block the headlock **(3-434)**, you can step your other hip in and throw him the opposite way **(3-435)**. You might be able to take him to the mat just by hipping in **(3-436)**. But if he doesn't go down, step your leg across and block his leg above his knee **(3-437)**. Make sure your weight is forward, and drive him over that leg **(3-438)**.

● **He has a bear hug.** If he is under both of your arms and is trying to bear hug you, sag your hips so you have space to get your hips through **(3-439)**. From here you can throw a head lock to either side **(3-440)**.

Figure 3-435

Figure 3-436

Figure 3-437

Figure 3-438

Figure 3-439

Figure 3-440

Finishes

When you land you should keep a hold on his arm with your one arm and post your other arm out so you don't get rolled through **(3-441)**. Once you've landed and adjusted your weight, you can lock your arms up. Your legs should be out perpendicular, your hips up. There are at least four ways you can finish it:

● Pull up on his head and his arm so he can't bridge **(3-442)**.

● Push his arm across his face **(3-443)**, hold it there with your head; then lock your hands again **(3-444)**.

● Push his arm to the side of his head **(3-445)**, holding it there with your head. Lock your hands again **(3-446)**, turn your hips down and drive your shoulder into his throat **(3-447)**. You can easily cut off the other wrestler's blood supply this way; so be aware of this.

Figure 3-441

Figure 3-442

Figure 3-443

Figure 3-444

Figure 3-445

Figure 3-446

Figure 3-447

● Hook your arm around his elbow and lift both his elbow and his head **(3-448)**.

If you don't get your hips through **(3-449)**, you have three options:

● **Restep.** Step back out and then back-step in again.

● **Sag Step.** Turn your palm up and toward the back to make it tighter. Set your inside leg out in front of you and put all your weight on his head **(3-450 to 3-451)**.

● **Block and trip.** You are in position to throw the move just as it was explained above **(3-452) (3-432 to 3-433)**.

Figure 3-448

If you miss or slip off his head, **(3-453)**, keep your momentum going, lock his elbow **(3-454)**, and throw him with his arm instead of his head **(3-455)**. Once you've taken him to the mat, you can either keep his arm or change to the headlock position **(3-456)**.

Figure 3-449

Figure 3-450

Figure 3-451

Figure 3-452

Figure 3-453

Figure 3-454

Figure 3-455

Figure 3-456

Shoulder Throws

Shoulder throw on your feet

Control either of his upper arms with your same-side arm. Reach your other arm across and hook under his shoulder and pull his shoulder tight to yours (3-457). Pull him so he steps behind you, back step toward the arm you have locked, and then finish the throw just as you did the headlock (3-458 to 3-459). You want to keep your shoulder *above* his and get your hips all the way through.

The same shoulder throw can also be made from an over-under hook. Pull him toward the underhook side, then release the underhook arm, reach it across to control under his shoulder, and back step at the same time.

Shoulder hit

On this throw, you are *not* going to get your hips through. From either of the over-underhook or else the control described above (both arms controlling his same arm), get him circling toward his free arm, then *hit* your shoulder into his, turn your hips down to the mat, and drive straight down to the mat (3-460). You will not land on him (3-461), but as soon as you hit, keep control of his arm (tight to your chest), and turn your hips up so your back is on his chest. You should be able to hold him here for back points.

Shoulder throw down to your knees

You can start with both arms controlling his same arm, from an over-underhook, or when he ties up with your head or shoulder (you reach over his elbow and pull his arm into your chest). You begin a normal backstep with your lead foot, but instead of bringing the trail-foot up toe-to-heel, step that leg back through his legs and drop to both knees (3-462). You will end up with your *back* to his chest (3-463). If you started with an over-underhook or by pinching his elbow to your chest, you have to reach your other arm under his shoulder as you backstep. Keep his shoulder tight to yours through the whole move and pull him straight over you (3-464).

Figure 3-457

Figure 3-458

Figure 3-459

Figure 3-460

Figure 3-461

Figure 3-462

Figure 3-463

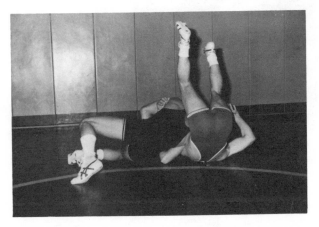

Figure 3-464

4
ESCAPES AND REVERSALS

There are a few fundamental rules that apply to almost all escapes and reversals. The first of these is to work from a good base. You can do very little when you're flat on your stomach; so whenever you get broken down you should get back to your base as described in the basic skills. A second basic rule is that you don't need to be completely broken down before you start your escape. Frequently when a wrestler is taken down he will go flat to his stomach, swear at himself, try to figure out what happened, and then—if he isn't already on his back—finally try to get to his base and get out. Instead, *as* a wrestler is being taken down or broken down, he should already be starting to escape. If an opponent has you three-quarters of the way taken down, you should consider yourself one-quarter of the way *out* and already be working to get totally out before you are totally taken down. As with all other positions, chain wrestling is important in escaping—if the first move doesn't work, *immediately* hit a second position. The third and most important point to escaping is always to have hand control. Getting hand control should be the first step in almost every escape. Without it, good position, effort, and all subsequent moves may simply be wasted.

Stand Ups

There are many types of stand ups, but there are two key points to all of them. The first is that you should get hand control *before* you start to come up. *Don't* come up to your feet first and then fight for hand control. The second point is that as you come up, you should drive your back *into* the man. *Don't* come up with your weight forward.

Getting to the standing position

● **Inside leg stand up catching his wrist.** As you step your inside foot up and drive back into the man, throw your inside arm up, reach under it with your other arm, and then grab his wrist **(4-1)**. Next, *without* taking a step with your outside foot, drive your back into the man and *pivot* up on your outside foot. As you are coming up, grab his wrist with your inside hand **(4-2)** and lock your arm straight so he can't bring his hand back. The leg that is on the same side as your arm that is controlling his wrist should be out in front of you; your other leg should be back; your back should be into the man, and your hips should be out **(4-3).**

Figure 4-1

Figure 4-2

Figure 4-3

Iowa's Barry Davis works for an escape from Iowa State's Mike Picozzi.

● **Inside leg stand up bringing your elbow back.** Step your inside foot up and drive back into him just as in the first stand up. As you step up, drive your inside elbow back into his chest, face, or whatever part of him is there to hit. Also as you're coming up, control the fingers of his hand that is around your waist **(4-4)**. Straighten that arm out and finish as in the stand up above.

● **Outside leg stand ups.** These can be done just as above, the only difference being that you first come up on your outside foot.

● **Feet out stand up.** This is a good standup if he is consistently beating you by picking your outside ankle. On the whistle, pivot on both knees and slide both your feet to the outside **(4-5)**. Your knees *don't* move at all. If he tried to pick your outside ankle, his hand will probably be somewhere on your outside leg. Grab his wrist with your outside hand, plant your feet in the mat, drive your back into him, and come to your feet **(4-6 to 4-7)**. Pull his arm forward so you keep his chest tight to your back and he can't suck you back underneath him. He still might try to set you on your butt. If he does, just hip heist toward his hand that you are controlling **(4-78 to 4-80)**.

● **He has your outside ankle. (4-8)** Reach back with your outside hand and grab his wrist. As you hold his wrist, rotate back over your foot that he has, and drive your back into him. This should free your ankle **(4-9)**. From here, keep a hold on his wrist and either push back into him and come all the way up to your feet, or else plant his hand on the mat, get your butt off the mat, and hip hiest to the outside.

● **Short sit directly to a stand up.** From a short sit out, with both feet close to your butt and planted in the mat, control his hand that is around your waist, and keep your other elbow in to your side so he can't reach under it **(4-10)**. Just as in the last two moves described, pull his wrist tight so your back stays tight to him. Turn his head away by driving your head into it **(4-11)**. By pushing back into him, you can come all the way to your feet or you can hip heist out at any level. If he tries to pull you back, hip heist out.

Figure 4-4

Figure 4-5

Figure 4-6

Figure 4-7

Figure 4-8

Figure 4-9

Figure 4-10

Figure 4-11

● **From a short sit out, post your hand (4-12)** (that's on the side where he is underhooked or around your waist) and bring your knee back underneath you **(4-13)**. All his weight is now on your side where he is underhooked, so he can't chop you down until he spins around to your other side where he is hooked over your arm. As he starts to spin around you, push back into him, and control his hand that's controlling your arm **(4-14)**. Once on your feet, change your hands that are controlling his wrist so you finish as above **(4-3)**.

Figure 4-12

Figure 4-13

Figure 4-14

Finishes to the stand up once you are on your feet

● From the standing position, with wrist control, your same-side foot out in front of you, your back into the man and your butt out **(4-15)**, you can simply step your back foot behind your forward foot **(4-16)**, controlling his hand until you are facing him. *Don't* worry about the hand that's around your waist. As long as you turn into it, he can't hold you with it. If you turn with it, then you will just be tightening his grip. If you remember to put your leg (the one on the same side where you are controlling his wrist) out in front of you, you just have to turn the way that is easiest: your back leg behind your forward leg, not the other way around.

● **Shear.** From the same standing position described in the last move, raise your arm so it's along the side of your head **(4-17)**. You're again going to step your back leg behind your forward leg, but this time slide your hips down and bring your arm down between his shoulder and head, *not* over his arm **(4-18)**. This is not a power move. You are simply sliding away from him.

● **Breaking his grip.** If he's behind you with his hands locked, there are several ways to break his grip:

a) Push his bottom hand with *both* of your hands down to the hip of your leg that is forward. Fight him 2-hands-on-1, not 1-on-1. Once his hands are down to your hip, throw your back into him and your hips out, breaking his grip **(4-19)**. You can also fight his top hand by cupping under his thumb and turning his hand up and out **(4-20)**. From here, the rest of the move is the same as if you were fighting his bottom hand.

b) If his hands are up around your chest, you can throw both elbows back against his forearms at the same time that you throw your hips out and your back into him **(4-21)**.

Figure 4-15

Figure 4-16

Figure 4-17

Figure 4-18

Figure 4-19

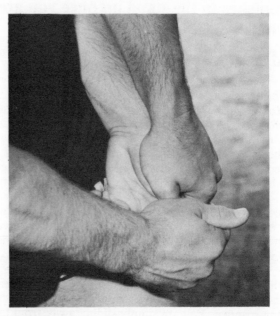

Figure 4-20

Figure 4-21

● If you can't break his grip, you can:

a) **Switch.** You want to have his leg on the side you are going to switch back so there is a space between your hips and his **(4-22)**. You can do this by walking forward and hitting the switch just as his leg is ready to follow forward but is still back, or by faking a switch to one side and then hitting it on the other side When you hit the switch, drive your elbow down hard on his arm, reach for inside his leg, and get your hips out **(4-23)**. You can go down to the mat, or stay on your feet to finish.

b) **Ankle Block.** Grab his wrist with your opposite hand. Walk forward, and as soon as he plants his foot, post your foot to the outside of it (as a block); then pull his wrist across and whip your hips down to the mat **(4-24)**. After you both hit **(4-25)** you can switch hands and come into a Peterson **(4-29)** or else turn toward his legs.

c) **Step behind his leg and Granby.** Again, you have to get space between your hip and the leg behind which you are going to step. One of the easiest ways is to walk forward and right after you take a step on one side, creating a space, then step your other leg behind his leg on that side **(4-26)**. Keep control of his arm that is around you waist, and with your other arm reach around the inside of his near leg **(4-27)**. From there just roll back **(4-28)** into a Granby (Peterson) position **(4-29)**.

Figure 4-22

Figure 4-23

Figure 4-24

Figure 4-25

Figure 4-26

Figure 4-27

Figure 4-28

Figure 4-29

d) **Throw.** Try to break his grip by fighting with both of your hands on one of his hands and driving your hips out **(4-19).** If you can't break his grip, bring your hips back quickly and to the side of his hips **(4-30).** Bring your forward foot back next to your other one, and you should be in a throw position (just as described for a head lock or hip toss after you have back stepped in). Your hips are *all the way* through, your knees are bent, your feet are parallel and about eight inches apart, and you are pulling his arm *tight* around you. All you need to do from here is straighten your legs and then pull his arm underneath you **(4-31).** When you finish, keep his arm and get your back on his chest.

Figure 4-30

Figure 4-31

Finishes From Behind the Man, On Your Feet

These are all finishes when you are locked around his waist without one of his arm locked **(4-32)**. If you have an arm locked, it should be easy to take him to the mat as long as you take him to the mat towards the side you have trapped (since he doesn't have a brace on that side.)

Figure 4-32

Keith Mourlam taking Mike Land to the mat.

● **Step to his side and lift.** Step around to either side, with your knees bent so your hips are below his and with his leg between your knees and tight to your hip **(4-33)**. In the same motion, lift him (using your legs, not your back) **(4-34)**, and take him to the mat **(4-35)**.

● **Fake stepping to one side and then going to the opposite side.** When you try the above throw, he will often step his opposite leg out and shift his weight to that side so you can't lift him **(4-36)**. To counter this, fake stepping around one side, (step only enough to get him to step with his opposite leg and shift his weight to it) and then take a long step **(4-37)** around to the opposite side so you are straddling his leg. Then finish as above.

● **Trip outside.** Step one of your legs around his same side leg. At the same time, unlock your hands and grab his opposite hip **(4-38)**. As you trip him forward, pull his hip through **(4-39)** and finish just as you do with the jam breakdown—setting him on his butt in front of you **(4-40)**. Make sure your head is *up* and your hand is only on his hip, not around his waist. Otherwise, he could switch you.

Figure 4-33

Figure 4-34

Figure 4-35

Figure 4-36

Figure 4-37

Figure 4-38

Figure 4-39

Figure 4-40

● **Trip inside.** Change levels (lower your hips by bending your knees) and step one of your legs around his opposite side leg **(4-41)** and trip him forward **(4-42).**

● **Snap back.** If he is standing straight up, lift him up and throw your hips into him to get his legs out **(4-43).** Then unlock your hands and come underneath both his arms. Hook your chin over his shoulder and pull him down onto his back **(4-44).**

Figure 4-41

Figure 4-42

Figure 4-43. Mark Trizzino sucking his opponent back.

Figure 4-44

● **Sag on thigh.** Bring your locked hands to either side so your hands are on his hip **(4-45).** Pry your forearm down on his thigh. You should be able to get enough pressure to take him down with it.

● **Sweeping his legs.** Lift the man up so his weight is off the mat. Then, use either knee to sweep his legs out by hitting and sweeping his same leg *above* his knee **(4-46).**

● **Pull back and block ankle.** Get your hips to one side of his hips but still stay *tight*. Block his ankle on the opposite side with your foot, then pull him back over it **(4-47).** He should land on his butt **(4-48),** *not* on you, and then you should come up on top of him. If you don't stay tight when you pull him back, he could switch you as you're going back **(4-49),** or after you hit the mat.

Figure 4-45

Figure 4-46

Figure 4-47

Figure 4-48

Figure 4-49

● **Leg tackle.** He has pushed your hands down low and is about to break your grip **(4-50)**. Lower your hips, unlock your hands and grab just below his knees **(4-51)**, then drive your shoulder into the back of his thighs **(4-52)**.

● He has broken your grip and has control of one of your hands out to his side **(4-53)**. Bring that hand behind him and through his crotch **(4-54)**. Keep the other hand around his waist. From here you can lift him and take him to the mat.

● **Shooting in on a single.** When he is almost completely out **(4-55)**, rather than letting him go, lower your hips and shoot in for a low single or double, as explained earlier **(4-51)**.

Figure 4-50

Figure 4-51

Figure 4-52

Figure 4-53

Figure 4-54

Figure 4-55

Sit-Outs

Short sit-out

From referee's position, post on your inside arm and outside foot **(4-56),** control your opponent's fingers and at the same time step the inside leg out **(4-57)** so you end up on your butt with both legs out in front of you and your opponent behind you **(4-58).** Your butt should be right under your shoulders - you shouldn't be leaning way forward where you can get cradled, or leaning back where you can get sucked back. Your knees should be bent and feet planted in the mat so you can push off them. If he tries to suck you back, get your butt underneath you. The arm not controlling his fingers should be in tight to your side so he has to reach over it. There are several finishes:

TURN

Still controlling his fingers, pull his hand up from around your waist to your armpit (so he can't lock around your waist and follow) **(4-59).** Go down to your opposite shoulder and at the same time, bring your outside knee up hard to your head **(4-60).** Still control his fingers while you're turning. Once you've turned in, go behind him if you've ended up far enough to his side. If you can't get around him, make sure the inside arm comes up to block him from going around you **(4-61).** If he puts his head or an arm over one of your shoulders, hook it with your same-side arm, then go down to you opposite shoulder and finish as just described.

Figure 4-56

Figure 4-57

Figure 4-58

Figure 4-59

Figure 4-60

Figure 4-61

GRANBY OR PETERSON

If you've sat and turned but didn't get your shoulders all the way through (4-62) keep control of his wrist with your hand, pull it up to your armpit, and reach between his legs and grab around his near leg (4-63). Turn your head and shoulders down and back towards the man's leg, as you are reaching for his leg. This keeps the man's weight high up on your shoulders rather than behind you, where he wants it. Finish by pulling his arm tight and rolling him to his back (4-64).

ROLL

Just as with the Granby, this move is best to hit after you've tried to sit and turn, but he followed you. As he follows you, pull his arm tight (the arm around your waist), then roll him, throwing his far leg behind you with your free arm and elevating his near leg with your inside leg. (4-65).

TURN WITH HIS HEAD

No matter what side of your head his head is on, post your arm (on the side where he has elbow control) and bring that same side knee back underneath you. As you bring the knee back, lower your shoulder on that side so that you get both your shoulder and your head underneath his chest (4-66). Then, throw your other arm over your head (4-67), catching his head, and taking him to his back (4-68).

HIP HEIST OUT

Described in the hip hiest section (4-78 to 4-80).

STAND UP

Described in the stand up section (4-10 to 4-14).

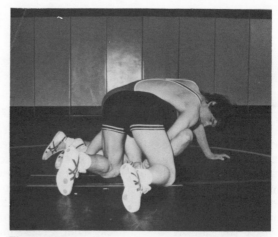

Figure 4-62

Figure 4-63

Figure 4-64

Figure 4-65

Figure 4-66

Figure 4-67

Figure 4-68

Sit back over the inside leg from referee's position (4-69)

Without moving your feet, lift your outside knee and sit *back* over your inside (4-70 to 4-72). You *don't* take a step forward with either leg. The entire movement is *back* into the man. As you sit back into him, control the fingers of his hand that's around your waist. This move is better than the short sit out because when you sit out, the man is on his toes behind you, ready and able to follow you. When you sit back into him, though, you should knock him back onto his butt (4-72). Pull his hand up to your armpit, go down to your shoulder, and turn into him, staying in a tight ball (4-60 to 4-61).

Figure 4-69

Figure 4-70

Figure 4-71

Figure 4-72

Sit back over the outside leg

This move works best when he is chopping your arm on the whistle and driving into you. You sit back over your outside leg and bring your near elbow back into your side, preventing him from getting under that arm (4-73 to 4-74). With that inside arm and your inside knee (which will be up after rotating over your outside leg) block his outside leg from stepping over your leg. You also duck your head, so that your elbow, inside knee, and head should all be together. It's important to rotate back into him and stay tight. If he is hitting into you hard, he will often go right over you. If he doesn't his arm should still be over your inside arm and you can just hook it and turn the opposite way (4-75), still staying tight and driving your knee up to your head.

Figure 4-73

Figure 4-74

Long sit out

Post on your inside arm and outside leg. Step your inside leg underneath the outside one and far out in front of you (4-76). Control his fingers. You can then either finish by turning into him (4-77) or else by hip heisting and turning away from him (4-78 to 4-80).

Figure 4-75

Figure 4-76

Figure 4-77

Figure 4-78

Figure 4-79

Figure 4-80

Hip Heist

The hip heist can be done from several positions, but the basic movement, (described in the basic skills section), is the same.

• **Sit-out to a hip heist.**—From a short sit out, control the wrist of the hand that is around your waist and pull it forward so his chest is tight to your back. Keep the elbow of your other arm into your side so he can't reach under it. Drive back into him so your butt is off the mat (4-78,) them hip heist into the arm that is around your waist (4-79). You should end up away from the man, not right in front of him (4-80).

• **Stand up to a hip heist.**—You can hit a hip heist at any level of the stand up. Just as with the sit out, turn into the arm that is around your waist.

• **Switch to a hip heist.**—If you get your hips out in a switch position but you can't finish the switch (4-81), hit the hip heist by stepping your outside leg under your inside leg (4-82).

• **Hip heist from referee's position.**—Do the move just as it is explained in the basic skills (2-5 to 2-7).

• **Hip heist to counter a double.**—As soon as the man sets you on your butt, you should post your arm that's on the same side as your leg that is between his legs, raise your butt off the mat (4-83), overhook his near arm with your other arm, then hip heist your inside leg under your outside leg (4-84). Finish by wizzering with your overhook arm. When you start the move, your inside leg should be between his legs, since if his knees are between your legs, the move is a lot harder. It's best to hit the move as soon as you hit the mat, but it can be used anytime you get into a similar position. You can also post your inside arm on his head rather than on the mat.

Figure 4-81

Figure 4-82

Figure 4-83

Figure 4-84

Mark Mysnyk illustrates a switch from the referee's position.

Switches

• **Referee's position.**—Just as with the hip heist, you want to get the man extended. To do this, step your inside arm forward and away from him. Step your outside foot up and plant it (4-85), then step your inside leg under it at a 45° angle away from him (4-86). You *don't* sit back toward his legs with your hips parallel to his. You want to get your hips away from him and get him extended. Once you've stepped your inside leg out, come over his shoulder with your arm and under his leg (4-87). Your butt *never* touches. You want all your weight driving his shoulder down to the mat. After his shoulder is on the mat, kick your inside leg over your outside leg and go behind him.

• **Switch to a hip heist.**—explained in the hip heist section (4-81 to 4-82).

• **Tripod switch.**—From the tripod position—You're on your hands and feet, with your knees off the mat (4-88), step your inside arm forward and away from him (to extend him), then step your inside leg out at a 45° angle and hit the switch (4-89). This move works very well if he is trying to chop your arm and his weight is forward.

Figure 4-85

Figure 4-86

Figure 4-87

Figure 4-88

Figure 4-89

• **Power switch.**—As mentioned above, you don't want your hips parallel to his when you switch. If you do get into this position while scrambling, though, and he steps over your foot, (block with your knee so he can't step across your whole leg), grab under your knee with your switch arm (4-90) and lift your leg to elevate him over to his side (4-91).

• **Inside switch.**—This move works best when he is bringing his arm that was on your elbow around your waist. You then lift your inside knee to make room for our outside leg, which you're going to step through at a 45° angle (4-92). Just as with the other switches, you want to get your hips away from him. Reach your inside arm over his shoulder and under his leg and switch him (4-93).

Figure 4-90

Figure 4-91

Figure 4-92

Figure 4-93

Rolls

With any rolls, never go down to your shoulders since he could half nelson you (4-94).

• **Same side roll.**—From a referee's position, grab his wrist and pull it tight across your waist. Roll to your hip, with your head up, and elevate his outside leg with your inside leg (4-95). Finish by keeping his wrist with your one arm and turning your hips down toward your legs as you drive your other arm under his far-side arm and then reach under his back (4-96). You can also finish with the Peterson or Granby by reaching between his legs and then around his inside leg.

• **Sit-out to a roll.**—Described in the sit-out section (4-65).

• **Turn inside.**—From a referee's position, step your inside knee back and drop your head down to your inside knee. Reach between his legs and then around his inside leg, putting you in the Peterson position (4-97). Hold his hand (that is around your waist) tight through the whole move, finishing with a Peterson (4-98).

Figure 4-94

Figure 4-95

Figure 4-96

Figure 4-97

Figure 4-98

Figure 4-99

• **Cross wrist roll.**—From referee's position or a tripod position, grab his wrist that is around your waist with your *opposite* hand (4-99). Post up on your outside hand and sit (whip) your hips under, without allowing them to touch until they are all the way through (4-100). Pull across on his arm at the same time and elevate his outside leg if it's still there (usually it won't be). You can finish with a head lock (by just reaching around his head with your free arm; a Peterson, by switching the hands that are controlling his wrist and reaching around his near leg; or turn towards his legs and come into his crotch with a navy ride.

• **Granby from referee's position.**—Post your inside arm, raise your hips and grab his wrist with your outside hand (4-101). Tuck your head toward the outside, step your inside leg under your outside leg (so he can't trap it), then go down to your inside shoulder (4-102) and kick your legs so they go right in front of your head (not straight over your back) and you roll across the top of your shoulders, not across your back. If he follows you, grab his inside leg on the way through and finish with a Peterson. If not, you should be able to roll all the way through. Keep control of his wrist (4-103) and spin around him for a reversal.

Figure 4-100

Figure 4-101

Figure 4-102

Figure 4-103

Figure 4-104

• **Granby from a sit-out.**—From a short sit, with your legs in close to your butt and planted so you can drive off them, again control his hand around your waist and roll to the side of which he has your elbow. Keep your elbow on that side in tight so he can't reach under your arm. For all granby's, it helps if he chops that arm—then go with the momentum. Finish just as above.

• **Granby from standing.**—With him behind you, in a standing position, you can do a granby just as from the sit-out position. Push off your inside foot, tuck your head, control the arm around your waist, and finish as above (4-104 to 4-105).

• **Elevate his outside leg.**—From referee's position, step your arm (that he is holding) forward and away from him to extend him. Sit back towards his legs, get your inside ankle under his leg (4-106), elevate him over to his side (4-107), then hip heist and finish with a half nelson (4-108).

Figure 4-105

Figure 4-106

Figure 4-107

Figure 4-108

All of the previous rolls were ones that you either hit or set up from referee's position. The following rolls are open depending on what he does:

• While still on your knees, drive your back into him and work for hand control. If he reaches over either side, grab his arm *above* the elbow with your same-side arm, grab his forearm with your opposite arm, and pull his arm down tight to your shoulder (4-109). You're now in the same position you would be in if you had hit a shoulder throw from your feet and went down to your knees. Finish by throwing your shoulder into him (4-110) and getting out perpendicular. You can just keep his arm tight to your chest and bridge your back onto his chest (4-111). You could also change to a headlock, a Peterson, or else post your head (4-112) and step your legs *high* across him (4-113). If you get parallel to him and he starts to put legs in (4-114), bend your knee to your chest, bringing his foot to you, then grab his in-step, throw his leg back over you (4-115), and get perpendicular again. Or, as he starts to put legs in, you can hip heist towards his legs.

Figure 4-109

Figure 4-110

Figure 4-111

Figure 4-112

Figure 4-113

Figure 4-114

Figure 4-115

Figure 4-116

• If he is riding you high with his outside knee up by your inside knee (4-116), grab the outside of it and lift it out and up as you drive your back into him. He will usually post his inside (or back) arm on the other side of you (4-117). When he does, reach around his arm, *above* the elbow (4-118), pull it down, and throw his leg behind you (4-119). You can finish it any of the ways described in the last move. If he doesn't post his hand on the other side, you can just lift his knee up, stand up, and turn into him.

• If he has a cross-face-far ankle ride on you, reach up with your arm and control his arm tight to your chest (4-120). Pull his arm down, drive your inside shoulder into him, post your head (4-121), and then step your legs over to the other side of him (4-122). The harder he is picking your ankle up, the easier it is to step over him.

Figure 4-117

Figure 4-118

Figure 4-119

Figure 4-120

Figure 4-121

Figure 4-122

• If he hooks over your inside ankle with his inside leg and is over your inside arm (4-123), rotate *over* your foot so it is flat on the mat and traps his leg. At the same time, throw your inside arm back hard around his waist (4-124). He will end up on his back and you will have your leg on top of him and between his legs (4-125). Post your other leg behind you so he can't roll into you, reach under his inside leg with one arm, and with the other arm you can reach around his head. If his leg and head are close enough, you can cradle him up with your leg still between his legs (4-126).

• If he hooks over your inside ankle and comes *under* your inside arm with his arm (4-127), pivot on your inside knee, lift your inside toe over his *outside* ankle and plant it there (4-128). Post on your inside arm and drive your hips into and then across him (4-129). You will end up in the same position as the last move (4-130). This move also works if he has overhooked your inside arm. The last move, though, *only* works when he is overhooked, not when he is under your inside arm.

Figure 4-123

Figure 4-124

Figure 4-125

Figure 4-126

Figure 4-127

Figure 4-128

Figure 4-129

Figure 4-130

5
BREAKDOWNS, RIDES, AND PINS

If done properly, each of these is hard to separate. A breakdown can lead directly to a ride or a pin, and conversely, a pinning combination such as an arm-bar or a one-half nelson is an excellent ride. Chain wrestling is important in each of these cases, and it is essential always to be aware of pinning opportunities since they often open up right after a takedown or in the middle of a flurry of moves. The importance of developing good pinning skills can't be over emphasized. Not only does a pin add extra points to the team total, it allows every wrestler, no matter how far behind, a chance to turn certain defeat into victory.

Dan Glenn works to breakdown his Iowa State opponent.

Breakdowns

● **Jam & Rotary Breakdown.** On the whistle, drive off both feet and hit under both his arms with yours and drive your chest into him **(5-1)**. This will break some men flat, but usually it will just stop your opponent's initial move. It's important that you are up on your toes, not your knees, so you can move easily. When you jam him, both your legs will be just behind him. After you've stopped his initial move, bring both legs to one side and block his knee with your inside knee **(5-2 to 5-3)**. Pry your outside arm on the inside of his far thigh **(5-4)**. As you lean back a little, use the thigh pry to pull him sideways over your knee and sit him on his butt right in front of you **(5-5)**. If you pry him back towards you he will end up on top of you rather than in front of you. From there you can break him down and go into a navy ride **(5-6)**, a bar arm **(5-24 to 5-25)**, a 1-on-1, etc.

Figure 5-1

Figure 5-2

Figure 5-3

Figure 5-4

Figure 5-5

Figure 5-6

● **Chop Near Arm.** At the same time you chop his near elbow and pull it back toward his waist, drive your inside knee up his crotch. This doubles him up and makes it easier for you to catch the hand you chopped with your other arm **(5-7)**. You can also use your arm that is around his waist to tight-waist him at the same time you chop his near arm. However, whenever you chop his near arm, be ready for him to switch you.

● **Rotary.** Hit under his near arm and drive it forward. At the same time, pry out the inside of his far thigh with the arm that was around his waist **(5-8)**. Run towards his head, and he will eventually break down.

Figure 5-7

● **Near Wrist.** Slide your arm down from his elbow to his wrist. Post his hand on the mat, then put your head in the back of his armpit and drive his shoulder over his wrist **(5-9)**, rather than pulling his wrist back. At the same time, pry out on his far thigh and circle towards his head to break him down flat **(5-10)**.

● **Cross face far ankle.** Cross face him so you have turned his head and are controlling his far arm above the elbow **(5-11)**. At the same time, pick his outside ankle and then drive him over. Keep control of his far arm even after you've broken him down **(5-12)** and look for a cradle or another pinning combination.

Figure 5-8

Figure 5-9

Figure 5-10

Figure 5-11

Figure 5-12

● **Outside "Ankle" Pick.** In referee's position, line up toward the back of him so you're closer to the ankle you are going to pick. Pick his outside foot at the laces (not the ankle) and change your other arm to around his waist. As soon as you pick his ankle, pick it up to his butt, get up on your feet **(5-13)**, and *run* him forward until he breaks down. Once he breaks down, trap his foot up to his butt with your thigh and keep it there and work for a pin. **(5-14)** If he moves his outside ankle before you can pick it, keep your hand moving across and pick his inside ankle **(5-15)**. Then, just as with the outside ankle pick, pick it up and drive him forward.

● **Inside ankle pick.** Pick the laces of his inside ankle with your hand that was on his elbow and finish as with the outside ankle pick **(5-16)**.

● **Knee block.** Pick his far ankle with the hand that was around his waist and reach over with your other arm and put pressure on his far shoulder so he can't stand up **(5-17)**. Then, chop his inside knee with your knee and pull his ankle forward at the same time **(5-18)**. Since your knee will end up underneath his thigh, you can finish by putting the legs in or else by pulling your leg out and coming on top of him. You can also use this breakdown to stop him from coming to his base after you have broken him down.

Figure 5-13

Figure 5-14

Figure 5-15

Figure 5-16

Figure 5-17

Figure 5-18

Pinning Combinations

Arm Bars

An arm bar is when you hook over one of the arms of your opponent with your same-side arm and put your fist on his back **(5-19).** The elbow of your bar arm should be holding his elbow in. *Don't* let him get the elbow of his barred arm out to the side.

Figure 5-19

Dan Glenn working to turn his opponent with an arm bar.

GETTING INTO THE ARM BARS

The most important thing for getting into arm bars is to be aware of them *all the time*. Some of the ways of getting into them are listed below, but it is certainly not an inclusive list, since in almost any situation you could put in a bar.

● Chop his near elbow with your same side arm **(5-7)**. As you pull it back, hook it with your arm and break him down. After he's flattened out, you can sink your arm in deeper and put your fist on the middle of his back.

● Chop his near arm with your same side arm, pull it back to his stomach, then grab it from his other side with your other arm. He will usually reach back with his other hand to free his wrist. When he brings up that elbow, hook under it with your other arm and pull it up on his back **(5-20)**. Then release his wrist with your other hand and bar his arm that you have underhooked **(5-21)**.

Figure 5-20

● Any time his elbows are out, you can put in an arm bar. If you've broken him down and he comes up to his base by doing a push up, with his elbows out **(5-22)** (instead of bringing a knee up and driving back over it), you can put in either a single or a double bar. If he usually comes to his base the right way, you can force him into coming up the wrong way by pinching his knees together with your knees **(5-23)** (so he can't bring a knee underneath him).

● **Head lever.** Grab his wrist and drive your head into his armpit **(5-10)**. After you've broken him down, bar him with your hand that has his wrist.

Figure 5-21

Figure 5-22

Figure 5-23

● **Jam and Rotary Breakdown. (5-1 to 5-3)** After you get to the position when he's in your lap **(5-24)**, put in a bar as you break him down **(5-25)**.

● **1-on-1**. Get a 1-on-1 on one of his arms, then bring your outside hip up under his arm to trap it **(5-26)**. Release the 1-on-1 and bar his arm.

● After you've broken him down, lock both your hands around the upper part of one of his arms **(5-27)**. Then, use both arms to jerk his arm (and therefore his elbow, too) up enough so you can put in a bar with your outside arm **(5-28)**.

Figure 5-24

Figure 5-25

Figure 5-26

Figure 5-27

Figure 5-28

TURNS USING THE ARM BARS

● You first have to tuck his opposite arm in so he doesn't have a post. Drop your elbow to the mat outside his arm **(5-29)** and scoop it back to his side **(5-30)**. Hold his arm there and drive your bar up towards his head and over his far shoulder **(5-31)**, *not* straight across his back **(5-32)**, since he could roll you through. If he has his head turned away and you can't turn him because he's blocking with it **(5-33)**, lift his near shoulder and head with your bar arm to take that post away from him **(5-34)**. Keep walking toward his head, with his arm that is barred trapped to your side, and your hips facing forward. As you are driving him, have your chest in his shoulder, not way over his back, so you don't get rolled through. If you do get too high, you can figure four his head and take him to his back with that. Once you have his weight posted on his far shoulder **(5-35)** you don't have to keep his arm tucked anymore. Instead, bring your arm (that was tucking his arm) back, and use it to replace your bar arm (put it under his arm and around his back) **(5-36)**. Take your bar arm out and use it to put in a half nelson **(5-37)**. Then get chest-to-chest and drive him over to his back.

Figure 5-29

Figure 5-30

Figure 5-31

Figure 5-32

Figure 5-33

Figure 5-34

Figure 5-35

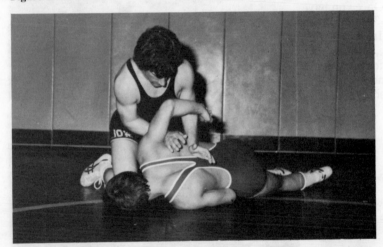

Figure 5-36

Figure 5-37

● You can keep the arm bar in, walk all the way around his head **(5-38)**, and then use your free arm to put a reverse nelson on him **(5-39)**.

● If he raises his elbow on the other side, underhook it with your free hand **(5-40)**. You can use the hook to pull his arm tight to his side and then run the bar as explained above **(5-41)**. Or, you can jerk his arm up hard **(5-42)** and then drive a half nelson on that far side **(5-43)**. You can either stay on the side on which you have the arm bar and stack him **(5-44)**, or you can jump to his other side and drive from there. You can use the half nelson to make him react and turn down his outside shoulder, and turn up the shoulder of the arm you have barred, making it easier to turn him with the bar. Or, you can try running the bar and then hit the half when he puts his inside shoulder down and his outside shoulder up.

Figure 5-38

Figure 5-39

Figure 5-40

Figure 5-41

Figure 5-42

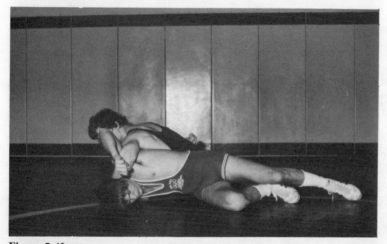

Figure 5-43

Figure 5-44

● You can step across his back, keeping the bar in, and hooking your outside heel in on his thigh as you go **(5-45)**. As you pull him toward his back, keep adjusting your hips up on top of him so you don't get them caught underneath him. Use your free hand to reach around the back of his head and grab his chin; then use that to help pull him toward his back.

● You can also step all the way across his back without putting the legs in **(5-46)**. Post your free arm across his head so he can't lift it, then circle around towards his head and change to a half nelson when you get around to the far side **(5-47)**.

● Use your free hand to grab his wrist. Turn his wrist in so it ends up palm out and it locks his arm so he can't bend it **(5-48)**. Drive his arm across his back, then step over his back with one of your knees **(5-49)**. You will now be sitting on his back with his arm trapped to the side of your body. You can take your bar arm out and start walking up toward his head. You can also stay on top of him and hook in the double grape vine after you turn him to his back, or you can step your other knee over to his far side too and put in a reverse nelson.

● If he comes up on his inside knee, step your inside knee in front of it **(5-50)**, pry on the inside of his far thigh, lift him over your knee, and stack him **(5-51)**. When he's flat on his stomach, the same type of move can be done if you can reach around his waist and grab his inside wrist. Keep his wrist as you stack him.

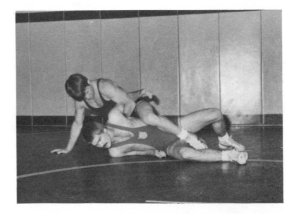

Figure 5-45

Figure 5-46

Figure 5-47

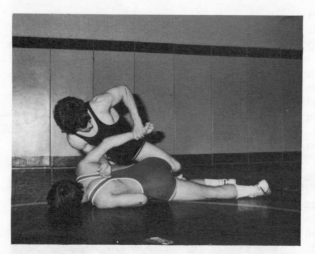

Figure 5-48

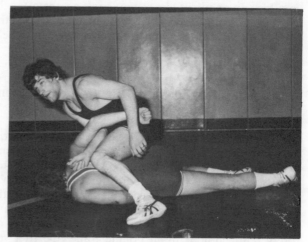

Figure 5-49

Figure 5-50

Figure 5-51

Near Wrist

As he is lying flat with his arms out in front of him, reach under his arm and grab over the top of his wrist **(5-52)**. *Drive* his body over his wrist **(5-53)** (rather than trying to *pull* it back under him) so it is under his chest or stomach. Reach into his crotch with your other hand and lift him onto your inside hip, while at the same time sliding your top foot under the instep of his bottom leg **(5-54)**. Change your hand from his crotch to his outside hip. Pull him over to his back, using the hand on his hip and lifting with the leg under his foot **(5-55)**. That leg will be bent. Use your knee to block his far thigh so he can't turn toward you. Make sure his thigh is on your hip, *tight* in your lap. If he does step over your block and turn toward you, slip your hand on his hip into a navy and bring your hips up **(5-56)**. You probably won't pin him with this move, but you should be able to hold him long enough for two of three back points. In free style, you don't have to hold him but can just roll him through. You can also use this move from referee's position by controlling his elbow instead of the near wrist. Pull his elbow back on the whistle and hold on to it. Pull him onto your hip and get your foot under the instep of his near foot at the same time. Then do the same move as above.

Figure 5-52

Figure 5-53

Figure 5-54

Figure 5-55

Figure 5-56

If he counters this turn by putting his inside hip up **(5-57),** pull his near wrist out from under him and walk around his head so your knees are straddling his head with your outside knee blocking his head **(see photo of Barry Davis).** When you walk toward his head, you have to keep weight and pressure on his near shoulder or head so he can't rise. Once you have his head blocked, straighten his arm and pull it directly toward you **(5-58),** not straight across his back. Once you have his arm up high enough, slip your arm that is closest to his legs between his arm and his side **(5-59),** and put in a half nelson with your other arm. Get chest to chest and drive him over. In free style, you can do it as above or just throw him through to get two points.

Figure 5-57

Figure 5-58

Figure 5-59

Barry Davis working to turn his opponent.

An Iowa wrestler has his opponent cradled up.

Cradles

FAR SIDE CRADLE

● If he comes up on his outside leg, reach across his face, under his far knee, and lock your hands (palm to palm, the way you lock when on a single leg) **(5-60)**. Step both of your legs over to that side and drive in to him to get him down on his outside hip **(5-61)**. Step your top leg underneath his knee and drag it forward, then step your bottom leg up to drive his leg up farther. Continue walking toward his head this way until he's ready to go over **(5-62)**. Then, step across him, your bottom leg first so your hips are down. Drive your bottom knee into his side, put your head into the side of his head, and use your other leg either to post with or to scissors his other leg **(5-63)**.

● As you reach over to lock up the cradle **(5-60)**, you can roll through **(5-64)**, taking him over your back **(5-65)**. Finish as above.

Figure 5-60

Figure 5-61

Figure 5-62

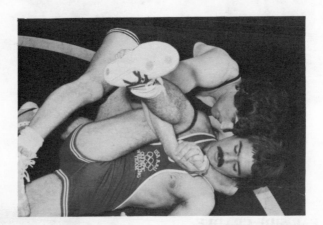

Figure 5-63

Figure 5-64

Figure 5-65

CROSS FACE CRADLE

The man is flat on the mat. Cross face him and control his opposite arm up high so your forearm keeps his head turned **(5-66).** Post your arm between his legs and then run around his head and drive his head to his knee **(5-67).** Don't try to bring his leg up to his head with just your arm. Keep a hold on his arm and lock your other hand onto that wrist. Sag back and finish just as with the far side cradle **(5-63).** If the man is up on a good base, cross face him and grab his far arm just above the elbow **(5-68).** Grab his far ankle, then circle toward his head, pulling his elbow up to extend him. He should end up on his butt with his foot planted flat on the mat **(5-69).** Keep a hold on his elbow, but release his ankle and put your hand underneath his foot. Drive his head down to his foot **(5-70),** grab your wrist, still keep a hold on his arm, and then take him to his back.

Figure 5-66

Figure 5-67

Figure 5-68

Figure 5-69

Figure 5-70

INSIDE CRADLES

You can get into this when he stands up with his inside leg first and gets his head near his knee **(5-71)**; or, if he is lying flat, put your head into his side, reach over his head and around his leg **(5-72)**, drive into him so he doubles up and then lock your hands. There are a number of finishes from here (man on his side).

● Run around his head and figure four his leg that you have cradled **(5-73)**. Plant your figure four leg on the mat.

● Scoop his top leg with your back leg **(5-74)** and then walk it around his head **(5-75)**.

● Scoop his top leg with your back leg, turn your hips forward and drive his knee forward enough so you can step your other knee behind his leg too **(5-76)**. Walk to his head and finish by lying across his head, hip down, posting on your head **(5-77)**.

● Pick up his top leg with your cradle arm so you can step your back or top leg underneath it and scoop his bottom leg **(5-78)**. Turn your hips forward and walk his leg up to his head **(5-79)**.

Figure 5-71

Figure 5-72

Figure 5-73

Figure 5-74

Figure 5-75

Figure 5-76

Figure 5-77

Figure 5-78

Figure 5-79

If he comes up to the tripod position **(5-80)** and you can't drive him over:

● Sit underneath him, your legs back toward his legs, pulling him on top of you **(5-81)**. Roll over your back then, pulling him over to his back **(5-82)**.

● Get both your knees to the outside of his leg so he can't elevate you **(5-83)**. Pick his leg up and take him straight back on his butt and to his back **(5-84)**. Post on your head and step both legs across his body **(5-85)** so you end up on top of him **(5-86)**.

Figure 5-80

Figure 5-81

Figure 5-82

Figure 5-83

Figure 5-84

Figure 5-85

Figure 5-86

LEG CRADLES

Scoop his inside leg and at the same time put a bar nelson on his head and far arm, using it to drive his head down to the mat **(5-87).** If you let him keep his head up, he can drive back into you, locking your leg with his, and reverse you as explained earlier **(4-123 to 4-130).** Once his head is planted on the mat, walk his inside knee to his head. When his head and knee are close enough, step over his head with your other knee **(5-88).** Pinch your knees together, then reach into his crotch and pull him over your knee **(5-89),** stacking him **(5-90).** If you can scoop his head with your front leg, you can put your feet together, arch your back, and walk your hands away from the man **(5-91).** You can do the same move if you are hooked over his far leg.

Figure 5-87

Figure 5-88

Figure 5-89

Figure 5-90

Figure 5-91

Legs

GETTING INTO LEGS

● One of the best times to put in a leg is after you have broken him down and he is coming back up to his base. Block behind his same side arm as you step the leg in so he can't grab your leg **(5-92)**. *Don't* lace your leg in so your knee is under him and your toe is hooked around his lower leg **(5-93)**. That takes away your post on that side, gives him an offense since he can roll over that hip and set you on your butt **(5-94)**, and takes away your foot with which you drive off. All you need is for your heel to be hooked as high up on his thigh as possible. Your knee should be to the outside of his hips where it acts as a post to keep him from rolling over his hip on that side. To break him down you can put your other foot under his instep **(5-95)** and pry out with that foot as you lift his other thigh with your heel **(5-96)**. You can also pick up his outside ankle with your hand and drive him to his side. If he starts coming back up to his base, either put your free foot under his free foot (instep) and pry out again, or else just push back with your free leg his knee that is coming up.

● Step over and block his far ankle with your back foot. Then drive your hips into him, hook his near shoulder, and drive him over to his side. As you are driving him over, hook your other leg in **(5-97)**.

● You can hook under both his shoulders, pull him back on top of you, and put the legs in then. This is not the safest way, though; moreover, instead of having him broken down you are on your butt, underneath him.

Figure 5-92

Figure 5-93

Figure 5-94

Figure 5-95

Figure 5-96

Figure 5-97

FINISHES

● **Bar Nelson.** Put the leg in on one side and bring your foot up on the other side so you are pinching his hips with your knees. Put the forearm across the back of his head and reach your other arm underneath his far arm and lock your hands **(5-98)**. The deeper you can sink your far arm, the better. Use your arm that is across his head to turn his head *away,* not down, and lift and turn his shoulder with your other arm. When you have broken him down to his side **(5-99)**, release the arm that's across his head and post on it. This allows you to raise your hips and sink your other arm deeper. Hold the little finger side of your fist across his head, not the palm side, since it's harder for him to bend your wrist this way. When you have turned him enough, step over to his other side and drive a half.

If you do the move when he's flat on the mat, the key step is still to turn his head away with the arm that is just across his head. The elbow of that arm should be on the mat, next to his head **(5-100)**. The rest of the move is the same. If he is flat and has his far side arm out in front of him and next to his head so you can't grab it as before, reach across with your near arm and grab his wrist. Reach under his elbow and grab your own wrist with your other arm **(5-101)**. The rest of the move is the same from here.

Figure 5-98

Figure 5-99

Figure 5-100

Figure 5-101

● Bring your free knee up to block his far hip **(5-102)**. Arch your back, lift his leg with your heel, and bring the heel of the leg that is blocking his hip to the toes of your other leg so he can't kick out. When he is ready to go over, stay heel to toe but walk your far side knee out so it doesn't get caught underneath him. Keep your heel and his leg up high, post with your outside arm and cross face or hook his shoulder with your inside arm **(5-103)**. If you hook his shoulder, drive your elbow to his ear. If he turns away, drive his arm down harder. If he turns into you, step your inside leg over his other leg and put in the double grapevine **(5-104)**.

● Scoop his inside ankle and then reach back and grab his foot. Once you have it, pick his heel up and hook your heel as high up on his thigh as possible **(5-105)**. Keep a hold on his foot as you cross face him with your other arm, and try to drive his head and heel together **(5-106 to 5-107)**. At the same time you're bending him like this, hook in your other heel and arch him over.

Figure 5-102

Figure 5-103

Figure 5-104

Figure 5-105

Figure 5-106

Figure 5-107

● If you have legs in and he is flat, grab a 1-on-1 on the far side and hook your foot over his far leg, between his knee and ankle **(5-108).** Shift your hips over to that side, reach over his near leg and under his far leg, therefore putting you in a navy ride **(5-109).** Lift his leg, keep the 1-on-1, and take him to his back **(5-110).**

● If he's sitting on his outside hip or he's flat and you can pick up his inside leg **(5-111),** hook his bottom leg above the knee. Adjust your heel as high as you can, cross face and arch him over to his back **(5-112).** From there, keep the cross face or hook his shoulder **(5-103).**

Figure 5-108

Figure 5-109

Figure 5-110

Figure 5-111

Figure 5-112

● If you get your inside leg hooked between his either intentionally or by mistake, (this happens when you counter his takedowns in certain ways) **(5-113),** you can either drive a half nelson on the far side **(5-114 to 5-115)** or else lock your hands around his far leg **(5-116)** and spread eagle him **(5-117).**

Figure 5-113

Figure 5-114

Figure 5-115

Figure 5-116

Figure 5-117

● **Crucifix.** Once you have him *broken down flat,* grab his far arm with both hands, turn his wrist out so his arm locks **(5-118),** then lift his arm up, turning him to his back. Don't put his arm behind your head until you have him turned so he's about halfway over **(5-119).** Once his hand is behind your head, you can lock around his head and take him over to his back **(5-120).**

● **Spread Eagle.** After you have a leg in, reach around his other leg and lock your hands **(5-121).** Lift up and out on that knee, so you are splitting him, and at the same time turn your hip into him **(5-122).** When you get enough pressure and/or pain, the man will go over. When he does, you can either use your free leg to push his leg apart even farther, or else you can post it in back of you and drive him toward his shoulders **(5-123).**

Figure 5-118

Figure 5-119

Figure 5-120

Figure 5-121

Figure 5-122

Figure 5-123

COUNTERS TO LEGS

● The first counter is not to let the man get his legs in at all. To do this, catch either his foot **(5-124)** or his knee as he tries to put the leg in, throw it behind your back **(5-125),** then turn the other way quickly to face him **(5-126).**

● **Mule kick.** This works best at just the moment he is putting his leg in **(5-127).** Kick your leg straight back and up in the air **(5-128).** Once his leg is out, bring your knee back *right next* to your other knee so he can't put the legs in again.

● Drive your inside hip forward and down, raising your outside hip up **(5-129).** Once his leg is out, come back to your base.

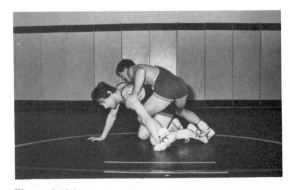

Figure 5-124

Figure 5-125

Figure 5-126

Figure 5-127

Figure 5-128

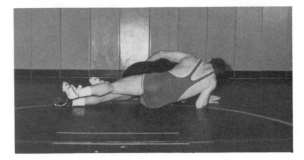

Figure 5-129

● If you can turn back to his ankles **(5-130)** and reach his far ankle, grab it **(5-131)** and drive into him **(5-132).** This will knock him down to his hip, and you should be able to come on top of him. When you turn back toward his ankles, turn with your head down and have your hand on your forehead so you can use your forearm to block his cross face attempts **(5-130).** If you have trouble reaching his ankle, you can drive your inside hip into him, making him bring his free foot in back of him as a post **(5-133).**

Figure 5-130

Figure 5-131

Figure 5-132

Figure 5-133

● **Somersault.** Come up off your knees **(5-134)** and then do a forward somersault **(5-135).** As you finish it, turn your hips into him and reach for his head **(5-136).**

● If he makes the mistake of hooking his leg in deep **(5-137),** turn your inside hip down, driving him to his hip **(5-138).** Post your inside hand so you can raise your hips and either drive up on his chest **(5-139)** or else get your hips out to the side of him **(5-140).** You are still in a scrambling position, but this is probably the best way to counter legs and will not only get you out of legs but also give you a reversal. If you can drive him over on his butt, but you can't get out from between his legs, you can:

1) **Fight for hand control.** You don't want him to be underhooked **(5-141),** since he can hold you in his lap then. Work on one side first **(5-142),** then hold that elbow in and work on the other side **(5-143).**

Figure 5-134

Figure 5-135

Figure 5-136

Figure 5-137

Figure 5-138

Figure 5-139

Figure 5-140

Figure 5-141

Figure 5-142

Figure 5-143

2) **Slide your hips down.** If you can reach under his leg **(5-144),** try to put it behind your head as you slide your hips down, and then turn into him **(5-145).**

3) **Step a foot across to his opposite ankle and step down on it to post it (5-146).** Once his foot is posted, he won't be able to use that leg to block you from getting your hips out. Post your hand and then raise your hips over that leg **(5-147).**

4) **Do a somersault straight back over his head (5-148), and try to grab his head as you are going over (5-149).**

5) **Grab across the tops of both of his feet and drive your forearms into his shins (5-150),** then slide your hips **down.** If you get the right pressure, this is very painful for the other man.

Figure 5-144

Figure 5-145

Figure 5-146

Figure 5-147

Figure 5-148

Figure 5-149

Figure 5-150

6
FREESTYLE TURNS

Most of the following turns can also be used in high school wrestling. Some of them are listed here because you expose his back - but he usually escapes after that (crotch lift). Others are listed here because they are illegal in high school (such as the gut wrench, because you are locking your hands). Except for the illegal moves, all of the following can be used to score in high school, and all of the turns you use in high school can be used in freestyle (as long as you don't roll across both shoulders doing the move).

Randy Lewis crotch lifting his opponent.

He's on his knees, in on your leg

● He's in on a single with his head to the inside. Block his inside shoulder and head with your leg (**6-1 to 6-2**). Grab his outside hip (*not* around the waist, since he could roll you), and pull him over your knee (**6-3**). You can finish in any of three ways:

1) Once you have exposed his back, let him get back to his base and you can try the same move again.

2) As you take him to his back, kick back hard on the leg he is holding (**6-4**), free it; then put in a reverse half nelson and hold him on his back (**6-5**).

3) If you can't free the leg he is holding; hook under his arm (**6-6**); then walk your leg back. If he holds on, he will go to his back (**6-7**).

In all the finishes, you should post your arm and stay on top of him. Don't go down flat on your side.

Figure 6-1

Figure 6-2

Figure 6-3

Figure 6-4

Figure 6-5

Figure 6-6

Figure 6-7

From referee's position (6-8)

● Hook his inside shoulder and pull it up enough so you can step your knee across his chest. At the same time, step your back foot across to block his outside ankle **(6-9).** Use both your shoulder hook and your knee to drive him back over to his back **(6-10).**

● **Crotch lift.** To start this move, you need to have both arms locked around his far thigh and your hip under his near hip **(6-11).** From this position, get off your butt and arch *straight* back towards his head **(6-12).** Don't break his back, but bend him enough so he wants to turn. Then, throw him over his inside shoulder **(6-13)** and come up to your base quickly to face him in case he tries coming back into you. If you can pull his outside ankle up to his butt and lock around it and his thigh **(6-14),** you can turn him easier. A third way of starting the move is to pick his *inside* ankle up to his butt and then trap it as you lock around his outside thigh **(6-15).**

Figure 6-8

Figure 6-9

Figure 6-10

Figure 6-11

Figure 6-12

Figure 6-13

Figure 6-14

Figure 6-15

● **Gut Wrench.** This move can be done with your arms locked only around his waist, but the move is even more effective if you can also trap one of his arms to his side so that he won't be able to brace with it **(6-16).** Just as with the crotch lift, you have to get his inside hip up on your hip. Your head should be flat on his back facing away from the direction in which you are going to throw him. When you do throw him, *don't* bring him straight across you. Bridge up *into* him and throw your hips into him **(6-17 to 6-18).** As long as you bridge you won't give away any back points. If you stay locked up, you can repeat this move as much as you want and score each time.

● **Leg Wrench.** When he's flat on the mat or as he's going flat, lock both arms around his thighs as tightly as you can **(6-19).** Lift his thighs into your chest and drive your shoulders into them to get his upper body flat on the mat. You can take him either way, but turn your head away from the way you are going to take him. If taking him to the left, step your right leg over your left leg **(6-20),** then bridge through and into him, keeping his thighs tight to your chest **(7-21).** Just as with the gut wrench, you can keep on doing this move continuously and score two points each time.

Figure 6-16

Figure 6-17

Figure 6-18

Figure 6-19

Figure 6-20

Figure 6-21

● **Leg Lift.** Pick his outside ankle up to his butt **(6-22).** If he is keeping his leg stiff so you can't pick it up, try to pick up the inside leg first, then drop it quickly and pick up his outside leg very fast. It will always be relaxed. Once you have it up, cover it with your chest and then drop down to his near ankle and wrap your arm around it, too **(6-23).** As you cover his ankles with your chest, bring your outside knee up tight to his ankle. Use your arms to lift his legs up enough to get your knee under his ankles, then use your knee to help lift his legs the rest of the way **(6-24).** Come up to your feet, but make sure he can't reach back to your feet and trip you back. Reach your other hand between his knees and grab the outside of his inside knee **(6-25).** Lever him toward his back, and when he turns **(6-26),** drop his knees toward his head and try to stack him or throw in a half nelson.

Figure 6-22

Figure 6-23

Figure 6-24

Figure 6-25

Figure 6-26

● When he's flat on the mat and you are sitting on him with your knees on both sides of him, hook over his shoulder on one side and bring your foot up by that shoulder **(6-27)**. Block his opposite hip with your knee, hold his shoulder tight to your chest, and then drive off your foot so that you are using your leg, not your arms, to lift his shoulder **(6-28)**. As you take him over, hook your leg in **(6-29)**.

You can do the same move by locking your hands around his shoulder and pulling him tight to your chest **(6-30)**. As you take him over your knee to his back **(6-31)**, adjust your hips on top of him and hook your leg in **(6-32)**. You can set this move up by starting to lift one shoulder, then when he drives that shoulder down to counter you, lift his other shoulder and go through the move.

Figure 6-27

Figure 6-28

Figure 6-29

Figure 6-30

Figure 6-31

Figure 6-32

● Pick up his inside thigh with both hands and put it on your hip **(6-33).** Once his leg is up on your hip, control it with just your inside hand and step your outside leg over to the opposite side of his head and plant it there **(6-34).** Lift his leg up even more and drive him over your foot **(6-35),** turning him to his back.

● If he's staying in referee's position to counter you, get to the side of him and reach your front arm in front of his inside thigh and grab on top of his far ankle. Both of your hands will be on top of his far leg, one just behind his knee and the other on his ankle **(6-36).** From this position, drive your shoulders into him and pull his outside leg to you, driving him to his back **(6-37 to 6-38).**

Figure 6-33

Figure 6-34

Figure 6-35

Figure 6-36

Figure 6-37

Figure 6-38

CONCLUSION

The advice and technique included in this book can certainly help make anyone an excellent wrestler. Being the BEST, though, requires mental toughness, described below:

Most men stop when they begin to tire.

Good men go until they think they are going to collapse.

But the VERY BEST know the mind tires before the body and push themselves further and further beyond all limits.

Only when all these limits are shattered can the unattainable be reached.

— Mark Mysnyk